TEAMBUILT

"If you really strive to create teamwork—and not just a close facsimile of it—this practical book will show you how to do it."
—Ken Blanchard
Co-Author, *The One Minute Manager*

TEAMBUILT

MAKING TEAMWORK WORK

Mark Sanborn

MasterMedia Limited · *New York*

134736

MASTERMEDIA and colophon are registered trademarks
of MasterMedia Limited.

Library of Congress Cataloging-in-Publication Data

Sanborn, Mark.
Teambuilt, making teamwork work / Mark Sanborn.
ISBN 0-942361-54-7
1. Work groups.   I. Title.
HD66.S257   1992
658.4'02—dc20

92-24054
CIP

10   9   8   7   6   5   4   3   2   1
Manufactured in the United States of America
Production services by Martin Cook Associates, New York

ACKNOWLEDGMENTS

This book would not have been possible without my clients who, over the years, have generously shared their ideas, experiences, and insights. Their trials and triumphs taught me a lot about teamwork. I'm grateful for the many opportunities I've had to work with truly teambuilt organizations.

I'd also like to express my appreciation to:

Michael LeBoeuf, Jeff Slutsky, and Robert Tucker for their friendship, encouragement, counsel, and support.

Francie and Marc Schwartz for sharing their expertise on teambuilding games.

Andrea Meyer for her research assistance.

Diana Lynn for her skillful editing and dedication to the project.

Susan Stautberg for her savvy publishing advice.

And finally, a special thanks to the business leaders and organizations featured in Chapter 13, "Developing the Teambuilt Difference," for their contributions to my work.

CONTENTS

Preface   ix

1   Teamwork Works   1

2   In the Beginning   14

3   Step 1: Locate   36

4   Step 2: Educate   49

5   Beyond Goal Setting   66

6   Clarifying Expectations for Exceptional Performance   77

7   The Attributes of Legendary Team Leadership   94

8   Step 3: Cooperate   113

9   Step 4: Communicate   129

10   Step 5: Motivate   151

11   Step 6: Celebrate   170

12   Taking the Team Through Tough Times   181

13   Developing the Teambuilt Difference   193

14   Continuing to Learn the Lesson of Teamwork   208

PREFACE

Teamwork is fast becoming one of the most compelling management philosophies in today's business world. Witness the recent explosion of books, articles, and seminars that tout the benefits of teamwork. Clearly corporate America has become more sophisticated in its thinking and writing about *teambuilding philosophy.* But what's missing is a corollary explosion in *teambuilding practice.*

I know this firsthand from years of experience as a business trainer, seminar leader, and professional speaker. Moreover, for the past six years I have extensively researched teamwork. I found volumes of information on teamwork theory but little on actual techniques for teaching people how to work as teams. Yet one of the biggest challenges most organizations face—and one of the greatest sources of frustration for employees—is the inability of leadership to effectively put theory into practice.

American companies, large and small, are recognizing the power of teamwork to increase productivity, inspire commitment and camaraderie, improve communication, and speed decision making. Teamwork can improve the performance and bottom-line results of almost any organization.

Take the San Diego Zoo. While much of Southern California tourism was suffering from the recession and Gulf War, the zoo—which is run by employee teams—was enjoying a 20 percent increase in attendance.

Zoo director Douglas Myers credits employees' sense of ownership: "I told them recession is coming; we're going to target our marketing on the local area alone, and we're going to ask all our visitors to come back five times—so each time they'd better have more fun than the time before.

"The employees came through," says Myers.

The growing use of teamwork is evidenced in the number of organizations competing for the new Quality Cup award. Developed by *USA Today* and the Rochester Institute of Technology, the award honors teams of 5 to 20 people in five categories: manufacturing firms, service companies, government agencies, nonprofit institutions, and small business.

More than 2,000 organizations and 431 teams applied for the 1992 awards—the competition's first. Entries ranged from major multinationals, such as IBM and Xerox, to nonprofit institutions such as the National Center for Missing and Exploited Children, to the Air Force's 18-man 37th Air Rescue Squadron.

"No matter what it is you're trying to do today, teams are the most effective way to get the job done," says Donald Petersen, former CEO at Ford Motor Co. and keynote speaker at the Quality Cup presentations.

Such testimonials win new converts by the droves. The problem is, too often teamwork success stories are long on inspiration and short on instruction. Missing are answers to the question most businesspeople ask: "How do we do it?"

That's what *Teambuilt* aims to teach.

You'll learn the 10 critical differences between a synergistic team and a traditional work group. I'll show you the six steps it takes to build a team and how to recognize team players from team slayers. *Teambuilt* is packed with practical advice, exercises, solutions to common problems, and even games, to help you make teamwork work.

Many of the concepts presented in this book will be familiar, because my aim was not to rewrite tried-and-true principles. What *Teambuilt* does is take these principles one step further to create a pragmatic business philosophy that combines theory and technique.

Does teamwork work for every organization? That depends on your expectations. *Teambuilt* can't promise to turn a failing business into an overnight success, but the lessons here will teach you how to have a more well-run operation.

Not every organization can achieve the kind of success required to become one of the media darlings that management gurus and business magazines routinely write about. If you and your organization aspire to such lofty heights, *Teambuilt* will point you in the right direction and, I hope, inspire you to get there. If you simply want to improve the quality of life for yourself and your people, and increase your organization's performance in the process, you've come to the right place.

—Mark Sanborn

TEAMBUILT

1

TEAMWORK WORKS

Teamwork works. That's the lesson being learned throughout corporate America, from the assembly line to the boardroom, and in organizations ranging from the military to nonprofit agencies to Fortune 500 companies. Teamwork works because it allows employees to take their jobs more seriously. It gives them a sense of control over their lives. It fosters commitment by getting them involved in the decision-making process, and ultimately, teamwork improves the bottom-line results of organizations that practice it.

The business media is full of examples of organizations that have proven the effectiveness of teamwork. Look at almost any successful group of people and you'll find high levels of teamwork—whether or not that's what they call it.

In 1986, for the first time, the U.S. Army discarded its traditional system of assigning soldiers to units individually in favor of a system that assigned teams of soldiers to units for their entire tour of duty. The Army found that soldiers who were part of a stable group were more productive, more reliable, and took more responsibility for the overall success of the operation.

Walmart is the largest retailer in America today, having sustained phenomenal growth for 25 consecutive years. One thing that distinguishes Walmart from its competitors is the depth of employee involvement. Walmart doesn't even refer to its employees as "employees"—they refer to them as "associates"; Walmart keeps associates informed of company policies and practices, and actively involves them in corporate decision making. Walmart is an unusual organization in that it isn't afraid of the NIH syndrome. NIH, which stands for "not invented here," is the tendency to resist any idea that you or the people in your department didn't think of yourselves. If you've been to a Walmart store recently, you probably noticed the store greeter who stands at the front of the store to welcome you and direct you to the area where you want to shop. This idea didn't come from the corporate marketing group; it didn't come from Walmart's customer service department—it was suggested by a cashier at a local store. The ability to get an idea that originates at a local level implemented throughout an entire retail system is testimony to the depth of employee involvement at Walmart.

Armor-All, the marketer of quality car care products, has only 65 employees. One of the best gauges of a company's productivity is sales per employee, a figure that is calculated by dividing total company sales by the number of employees. At Armor-All, the sales per employee is an impressive $2.4 million. How does Armor-All do it? Chief Executive Officer Jeffrey Sherman says, "I think teamwork is the key ingredient in our company's success. When you've only got 65 people and you're enjoying revenues of $2.4 million per employee, that must mean that people work together pretty well."

Another example of the power of teamwork is Japanese Air Lines. JAL used to maintain its aircraft much the same way American airlines do: a team of mechanics works on literally dozens of different airplanes in the course of a given year. In 1985, after experiencing one of the worse air disasters in history, JAL changed the way it maintains aircraft. At the airport just outside Tokyo, 15-person teams are assigned to only two aircraft: a DC10 and a 747. Inside every passenger cabin hangs a plaque signed by members of that plane's maintenance team. They also have implemented an unusual quality-control technique: after every major repair, the team leader has to fly on the airplane's first flight to make sure that the work was done right.

Stories like these prove the need for and effectiveness of organizational teamwork. Maybe that's why Rosabeth Moss Kanter, a consultant and professor at Harvard Business School, says, "In the 1990s, organization—the team—is the competitive weapon."

A 31-member commission created by the Labor Department reported in July 1991 that schools must start teaching such cognitive skills as teamwork if new workers are going to be equipped for the demanding jobs of the future. The commission also found that more than half of young Americans leave school without the skills needed for meaningful employment. Educators and employers clearly have their work cut out for them.

Today many of the most successfully managed companies in America credit their results to teamwork. These teambuilt companies include Boeing, Caterpillar, Digital Equipment, General Electric, and Proctor and Gamble, just to name a few. Teamwork makes sense to these successful organizations because they've found it can impact practically every aspect of performance. What follows are some of the benefits that can be achieved from the teamwork approach, with real-life examples of companies that have achieved them.

Increased Productivity

At a General Mills cereal plant in Lodi, California, teams schedule, operate, and maintain machinery so efficiently that the factory runs without managers during the night shift. At its Carlisle, Pennsylvania, plant, which makes Squeezit juice, teams changed some equipment and squeezed a 5 percent production increase out of a plant management thought was running at full capacity. General Mills says productivity in its plants using self-managed teams is as much as 40 percent higher than at its traditional factories.

Teams of blue collar workers at Johnsonville Foods of Sheboygan, Wisconsin, helped CEO Ralph Stayer make the decision to proceed with a major plant expansion. The workers told Stayer they could produce more sausage, faster than he ever dared ask. The company has gone from $15 million in sales in 1982 to $130 million in sales today.

Says Stayer, "The strategic decision is who makes the decision. There's a lot of talk about teamwork in this country, but we're not set up to generate it. Most quality circles don't give workers responsibility. They even make things worse. People in circles point out problems, and it's someone else's problem to do the fixing.

"When I started this business of teams, I was anxious to get it done and get back to my real job. Then I realized that, hey, this *is* my real job."

Better Decision Making and Problem Solving

Workers in companies with shared decision making tend to be more satisfied with their wages than employees of companies without team efforts—even if they aren't paid more, according to a survey of 4,565 Indianapolis employees conducted by sociologists at Wright State.

At a weekly team meeting, Federal Express clerks spotted—and eventually solved—a billing problem that was costing the company $2.1 million a year.

Improved Service

Infiniti has one of the largest, most extensive training programs in the history of the automobile industry. Most automobile salespeople see their job as "closing the sale." But Infiniti has retrained its dealers to see themselves not as salespeople, but as facilitators who help customers make informed choices by demonstrating the product knowledgeably. To reinforce teamwork within a dealership, Infiniti breaks down the traditional barriers between department managers by forcing them to focus not on a sales problem, a service issue, or even a parts question, but solving the customer's problem.

Morris Savings Bank in Morristown, New Jersey, has a program that rewards employee teamwork on retail accounts. Called Fas-Track, the program has changed employees' attitudes about selling. Instead of rewarding only account salespeople, it focuses on the teller's role in providing the kind of service that encourages customers to stay with the bank. Specifically, tellers are trained to be more sales-oriented and to suggest different bank services to customers.

Historically, organizations have believed that if you cut back on staff, you cut back on service and quality. Yet, after organizing its home office operations into superteams, Aetna Life & Casualty reduced the ratio of middle managers to workers from 1 to 7 down to 1 to 30—all the while improving customer service.

Innovative Marketing

In 1987, Rubbermaid began to develop an "auto office," a plastic, portable device designed to strap onto a car seat, hold files, pens, and other articles, and provide a writing surface. To research the concept, the company assembled a cross-functional team that included engineers, designers, and marketers, who went into the field to ask customers what features they wanted. The team members each asked questions from a different point of view. The result:

Rubbermaid brought the new product to market in 1990 and sales are running 50 percent above projections.

When Beech Aircraft Corp. needed an aggressive marketing program to capture its share of international business, the firm adopted a team approach to servicing the global market. They divided the world into three geographical areas and assigned a team to each. Teams make presentations directly to the president on a quarterly basis, and the decentralization has provided a powerful competitive edge.

Feedback and Conflict Resolution

Herman Miller, Inc., the $800 million office furniture manufacturer, was ranked ninth overall in *Fortune* magazine's 1989 survey of the most admired companies in America. All employees are organized into work teams. Every six months, team leaders evaluate their members and members get to evaluate their leaders. They also elect representatives to meet with line supervisors to discuss problems. If employees don't like the results of these meetings, they can bypass supervisors and go directly to the next executive level.

At Eastman Kodak Co., cross-functional teams are working together more smoothly and mediating their own disputes in a fraction of the time it once took.

Fewer Rules, Policies, and Procedures

Dana Corp. burned 21-inch-thick policy manuals. They eliminated reports and signoffs, and installed trust.

A team of employees and management redesigned the X-ray-testing process at Sentara Norfolk General Hospital, cutting it from an average 72.5 hours to 13.8.

The message is clear: For some of America's best companies, *teamwork works!*

WHY TEAMWORK?

Teamwork has always worked. One reason organizations are interested in teamwork is its potential to positively affect the bottom line. *Business Week* reported that companies are willing to undergo radical change in the way they do business so they can enjoy the benefits of their workers' commitment and expertise—not to mention productivity increases that, in some cases, exceed 30 percent.

Teamwork offers the classic double win: not only does the employer profit, but employees benefit as well. Teamwork takes employees seriously, gives them more control over their work lives, and creates commitment by getting them involved in the decision-making process. When these things happen, the bottom line is almost certain to improve.

Why, then, is it so hard for organizations to practice teambuilding? In the 1950s, Anthony Jay wrote a book called *The Corporation Man* that described how working in large organizations is a relatively new development. For thousands of years, our ancestors worked as hunter/gatherers, traveling in small groups of 9 to 12 people.

Being a hunter/gatherer is not a career opportunity many of us would opt for today. But there are at least three things we can learn from our ancestors' way of "doing business." First, there were no hunter/gatherer job descriptions. If you had good eyesight, you became the game spotter. If you were a fast runner, you chased the game. If you had more brawn than brains, you got to wrestle the game to the ground and kill it. In other words, you simply did what you were best at or whatever needed to be done.

Secondly, hunter/gatherers weren't burdened by memos. If you saw that your friend Trog was about to be eaten by a saber-toothed tiger, you simply yelled, "HEY TROG, LOOK OUT!" and ran. But in today's organization, you'd have to send a memo that might go like this:

> TO: Boss
> FROM: Cro-Magnon Bob
> RE: Trog
> It has come to my attention that Trog is about to be
> eaten by a saber-toothed tiger.
> Please advise.

Bob's boss would then send a memo to Trog's boss. By the time they got to Trog, he might be partially digested. (Just to show you how warped managers have become, I actually had a guy at a seminar in Tulsa tell me, "Yeah, but you could have *faxed* the memo.")

Thirdly, and curiously, hunter/gatherers worked very hard even though they didn't get paid or have titles. Status wasn't an issue. The real payoff was that if you did your job, you got to eat. To hunter/gatherers, results were more important than rank and success was more important than status.

Then, about 130 years ago, we entered the Industrial Revolution. Suddenly, employees were asked to work in groups of hundreds, and in some cases, even thousands. Communication became more difficult because of the hierarchy of the organization. Even more devastating, it became increasingly difficult for employees to see the linkage between their work and the results their organization enjoyed. A sense of camaraderie was lost and most of the good stuff learned from thousands of years of being hunter/gatherers was eliminated.

The moral of this story: *If you want to be leading edge in the year 2000, you need to de-evolve several million years.* Get rid of job descriptions that don't reflect talent or need. Make communication direct and fast. Create linkage between reward and performance. In short, practice the ancient and nearly lost art of teamwork.

Why Now?

If the team concept is a time-honored, proven tradition, why hasn't it been embraced by business sooner? One reason is that in business there is often an incredible lag time between when an idea is recognized as being useful and when it's widely adopted.

Consider this "news flash" from *The Wall Street Journal.* An item in the September 12, 1989, "Labor Letter" column says: "Wandering draws rave reviews as a management tool. You can't find out much sitting in your office. Wandering should include contact with both customers, as well as workers." Yet this concept—management by wandering around—was first made popular in 1982 by Tom Peters and Bob Waterman in their book *In Search of Excellence.* (Peter Drucker was using different terminology but talking about the same thing almost 20 years earlier.)

If the *Journal* is any indication, there was a seven-year lag between the time the concept was introduced and when corporate America took serious notice of it. Is it any wonder then that the age-old concept of teamwork has taken so long to become popular in organizational management?

Barriers to Teamwork

Teamwork has not been more quickly adopted because it faces significant barriers inherent in the work force. One of the biggest is that *most of us haven't been taught how to cooperate.* From the time kids enter grade school until they graduate with advanced degrees, a big part of their socialization experience is competitive activity in academics and sports. This continues in the workplace. (When was the last time you read a news release that said somebody was made V.P. because he or she ". . . did an exceptional job of helping coworkers and colleagues get ahead"?)

We learn at a very early age that if you're going to win, you've got to beat somebody to do it. Competition is linked to success. So we learn to ignore the unsavory aspects of competition: competing against friends and sometimes our own team members, stress, feelings of inadequacy and isolation, and in extreme cases, ruthlessness. (Maybe that's why a wise thinker once observed that competition doesn't develop character, it exposes it.)

To make teamwork work, we must reexamine our beliefs about competition. Alfie Cohen did an exhaustive study of research about competition that culminated in a book called *No Contest: The Case Against Competition.* Cohen spent more than five years studying the effects of competition on performance in the classroom and other organizations. He concluded, based on some 400 psychological studies, that *optimal productivity not only did not require competition, it usually required the absence of competition.* For instance, research in the classroom showed that when children were freed from the anxiety of competing with each other, their self-esteem increased markedly. Similarly, Cohen found that in the workplace when people started working together, rather than working against each other, productivity increased dramatically.

Making the Shift from Competition to Cooperation

To conclude that competition is bad would be a sweeping and invalid generalization. The real issue is how competition can be used to affect organizational performance. We need to harness healthy forms of competition to make teamwork work.

One way to increase self-esteem among team members is to get them to quit focusing on how they compare to others and start focusing on how they compare to their potential. That will eliminate the anxiety that hampers performance both in the classroom and in the workplace.

Seek out and change the things that discourage cooperation in your organization. One of my favorites: structured pay systems. Let's say that at the beginning of the year employees are told, "This year, 10 percent of you will qualify for a 12 percent increase; 30 percent of you will receive a 7 percent increase; and the rest of you will stay at your present level." Then, almost as an afterthought, company management says, "Now let's all work together." But that doesn't make much sense when you've got to beat 90 percent of your team members to receive the best pay increase. Such systems discourage teamwork.

Another common demotivator is "Employee of the Month." Conceptually, there's nothing wrong with recognizing a top performer each month, but the problem is that in most organizations, that's the only form of recognition given. So say you've got 60 people in your organization, and the only award you give is Employee of the Month—that means you have one winner and 59 losers every month. Doesn't it make more sense to create recognition programs that develop 60 winners? We need to get a lot better at recognizing *everyone* for their contributions, and later, I'll explain another approach for you to try.

Wanted: Better Role Models

Who are your teamwork role models? I've asked hundreds of seminar attendees, and their responses invariably include sports teams. I have nothing against professional sports, but in organizational teambuilding the sports analogy has limited use and meaning, for these reasons:

- Your team members don't get paid what professional athletes get paid.
- They don't get to practice more than they play.

- Their game lasts more than three hours.
- The rules your team plays by are probably changing while the game is in progress.

Granted, some good lessons can be learned from sports, but we've got to find new role models for building teams in our organizations.

Start searching out non-sports role models. Keep a file of newspaper and magazine articles about successful team approaches used by business, nonprofit organizations, the arts, science, and the public sector. After you've identified some role models, arrange to interview one.

The odds are stacked against teamwork. Despite our hunter/gatherer heritage, we have to overcome:

- the myth of competition
- systems that seldom reward teamwork
- a lack of good role models.

CREATING A TEAMWORK LABORATORY

Literally every area of your organization can be improved using the team concept. You may want to start by creating a teamwork laboratory for your organization. Let me explain how to do that.

Pick One of These Areas:

- productivity
- problem solving
- internal or external service
- marketing
- communications
- conflict resolution
- administration

Next, Quantify Your Current Level of Performance in That Area.
To determine how well you're doing, take something that's difficult to quantify, such as conflict, and ask yourself, "How quickly do we resolve conflicts? How satisfactory are the outcomes to all involved? What is the aftermath once the conflict has been resolved?" Your answers will form a baseline for comparison.

Your Next Step Is to Determine a Time Frame. Since you'll only be addressing one area, rather than moving your entire organization to team-based operations, 6 to 9 months will be feasible; 12 to 18 months would be even more realistic. Now, for that particular area, create a team approach with results you can measure during the time frame.

Evaluate the Results. Compare the team's performance with the baseline you established at the beginning of the experiment.

Assess Responsibility. If the team has not improved results in the area you've addressed, don't necessarily blame the team—because there's overwhelming evidence that teamwork can improve almost any area of operation. So the question becomes, "If performance didn't improve, what went wrong in implementing the teamwork?" Don't automatically assume that teamwork is an invalid concept. Rather, go back and look at your test to find out where you failed to truly implement the team concepts necessary to create an improvement in performance.

2

IN THE BEGINNING

You've read this far—and you must have some interest in the subject or you wouldn't have picked up *Teambuilt*. Chances are, I'm preaching to the converted, so I don't need to sell you, the reader. My objective is to show you how to sell your employees, coworkers, and managers—the real hard sell—on teambuilding. Chapter 1 included examples of organizations that are teambuilt and identified the barriers you'll have to overcome. Use those stories—and others like them that you find in your study of teambuilding—to make you a persuasive salesperson of the teambuilt philosophy.

You'll need all the help you can get, because frankly, your colleagues are skeptical. You say "teamwork" and they hear "gimmick." Here are some other definitions I've developed to help you prepare for the skeptics.

> ### THE SKEPTIC'S GLOSSARY
>
> **Teamwork:** another management fad that attempts to get employees to do more work without paying them for it.
> **Team Leader:** the boss.
> **Team Members:** the people who carry out the boss's orders.
> **Employee Involvement:** a technique that creates the illusion that management really cares about what I think.
> **Participative Management:** an opportunity to agree with what management has already decided.
> **Conflict:** a disagreement with management.

Faddish or gimmicky management techniques, and leaders who have been fickle in their attempts at organizational change, have given employees good reason to feel skeptical. But there has never been a management fad that employees didn't think they could outlive. The thinking goes something like this: "Management must have read the latest book on (choose from: excellence, quality, service, management, leadership, innovation). That means we'll be on a _____ kick until (choose one): a. management loses interest, b. they read another book that catches their fancy, or c. they give up because it didn't work. I'll listen politely, sit through their seminars, and wait it out like I've always done."

I don't care if you adopt my phrase "teambuilt." You can call it teambuilding, teaming, or synergistic partnering, or create a term of your own. What's important is that you commit to the timeless, changeless truths that are the foundation of the teambuilt concept. The ideas you'll find in the following pages aren't new, but I hope my approach, models, and presentation will be fresh. Still, the basic concepts should ring familiar for one reason:

Fads come and go, but truth is truth.

My premise is that while the philosophy of teambuilding isn't new, the practice of teambuilding is still practiced by a minority. Most managers understand the concepts—they just don't utilize them. Lack of information and knowledge about teamwork is not a problem in the vast majority of organizations I work with. What's missing is a practical application of the principles.

> *The difference between excellence and mediocrity is the difference between common knowledge and consistent application.*

Creating teamwork is hard work. It means committing to what you intuitively and quantitatively know is true, then staying the course—because the payoff justifies the cost.

DEFINING THE TEAM

Let's begin by defining what we're trying to create and how the team differs from traditional work units.

> *A team is a group of diverse people, united by a common purpose, who are cooperating to achieve quality results and experience synergy.*

There are four key components in that 23-word definition: diversity, cooperation, mission, and synergy.

Diversity

A team consists of people with different skills and abilities. Those are the most obvious differences. But we live in a richly diverse culture that brings together people of different age, race, gender, sexual orientation, marital status, religious beliefs, and educational background. Some of those differences are changeable; others are not. The key to making teamwork work is not conformity, but blending—capitalizing on the team's diversity.

Suspend reality for a moment and consider the following two scenarios:

Scenario A. You work with people who are exactly like you—same likes, same dislikes. They have identical interests, skills, and weaknesses. It's a predictable work environment because, to the degree you know and understand yourself, you know and understand your teammates.

Scenario B. You work with people who are all very different than you. Different likes and dislikes. Different interests, skills, and weaknesses. You can never be sure what anybody is thinking—without asking—so there's little predictability in this work environment.

Given a choice between those two scenarios, which would you choose? Be honest. Don't answer on the basis of how you think you should.

When I survey my client audiences, only a handful of people—no more than a dozen out of every 100—vote for Scenario A (and most of those do so hesitantly). The vast majority always vote for Scenario B.

This outcome is significant. It means those who chose Scenario B have concluded, "I would willingly accept a scenario that creates all of the conflict, all of the problems, and all the difficulty in building teamwork. Given a choice between reality and fantasy, I'll still take reality."

The blessing of teamwork is the curse of teamwork.

The curse is that everybody we work with is different; they bring different strengths and weaknesses to the team. But this is also the blessing of teamwork because the central strength of any team is its diversity and nonconformity.

It is regrettable that many efforts at teambuilding are misguided because they focus on getting team members to conform. Some team leaders recruit, hire, and train so that everyone is pretty much the same. And then they can't understand why the team lacks vitality. The next time you're frustrated at your inability to get along with or motivate another team member, remember that, despite this challenge, you probably still want the differences.

Cooperation

The concepts of common purpose and cooperation cannot be mutually exclusive because the definition of cooperation is "working together with others for mutual (often economic) gain." It doesn't mean losing your identity to the group (a concept I'll cover later). Cooperation focuses on how we act and interact with others and the motivation we have for doing so. The motivation for mutual gain in teams comes from a shared mission.

Mission

The German philosopher Friedrich Nietzsche said, "He who has a reason why can bear almost any blow." He believed a sense of purpose in life is even more important than what we do or the circumstances we experience.

Yet, in conversation, people typically ask, "What do you do?" The more important question is, *"Why* do you do it?"

Most organizations are the same way. Even if management has determined the "why" behind the "what," they seldom take time to communicate it to employees. Teams need to be able to answer the question, "Why does this team exist?" The key to teamwork is getting people to understand not only their goals, but the reasons why they should achieve those goals. Equally important, those reasons should represent mutual gain for both the team (organization) and team members (employees). If they don't, there is no common purpose.

Goals are often overrated as a motivational device. We can set goals for others, but without reasons to achieve those goals, they will not be motivated. Team leaders must be able to provide, or help their teams identify, reasons that they find motivating. Team leaders know:

> *The motivation is in the mission;*
> *the power is in the purpose.*

Synergy: The Acid Test of Teamwork

"In Pentagon parlance, the new buzzword for winning wars is 'synergy,' " began an article in *The Washington Post.* The December 20, 1991, article goes on to talk about a new 80-page publication that will be sent to all military officers, and enlisted men and women, in an effort to create cooperation among the highly competitive service branches. Army Col. Pete Herrly, who helped write the report, says, "This is a new American way of war. Teamwork is designed to result in 'synergy,' which means that the whole becomes greater than the sum of its parts."

The single most important aspect of teamwork is synergy.

> *Synergy occurs when the total or whole is greater than*
> *the sum of the individual parts*

> or

> *2 + 2 = 5 . . . or more!*

Here's a quick test to find out whether you have a team or work group. If you've got five people in your group producing the output of five people, you've got a loosely organized group. But if your group of five is producing the work of six—or even seven or eight—people, you've achieved synergy and created a high performance team.

A Winning Exercise

It's not enough for people to buy into synergy intellectually; they need to experience it firsthand if they are going to replicate it in their work. Here's an exercise you can use to help your group experience synergy. Just follow this script.

First you say: "Take a blank piece of paper and draw a line down the middle. At the top of the page write the words 'Styrofoam cup.' Don't worry about spelling Styrofoam correctly—this isn't a spelling exercise. In the next two minutes, working independently, make a list in the right-hand column of as many ideas as you can think for how to creatively use a Styrofoam cup. Be as creative as possible. The objective is quantity, not quality. You've only got two minutes, so work as quickly as you can. Go!"

At the end of two minutes tell them: "Please stop. Count your ideas and write that number at the bottom of the column. Now here's the second part of this exercise. Team up with two other people. PLEASE DON'T DO ANYTHING UNTIL YOU ARE IN YOUR TEAM OF THREE."

Wait briefly for that to occur, then continue: "You now have two minutes to work as a team to think of creative uses for a Styrofoam cup. At least one of you needs to list the ideas in the left-hand column. It is OK to use what you've already thought of individually, so you can begin by combining lists and building from there. Time is critical. Go!"

Stop at the end of *1 minute and 45 seconds*. Tell your group: "Please stop. Count up the total number of ideas you generated as a team, including the ideas you already had." (Give them time to count.) "Now, please answer these questions with a show of hands:

1. "How many of you, as a team, came up with more ideas than you had working individually?" (The response should include everybody. If not, you've got a real problem.)
2. "How many of you came up with an idea that none of you had until you teamed up?" (The point is that by working together, the teams generated new ideas.)
3. "Did you realize that I actually reduced the time you had to work?" (Most will be surprised.)
4. "How many of you would say you had more fun working together than alone?" (You should see a healthy show of hands because energy is *always* higher for the second part of the exercise.)

Tell the group: "What you've just experienced is synergy. Synergy allows you to get more done, have better ideas, in less time, and have more fun doing it."

The final step in this exercise is to reveal a flip-chart or overhead transparency with these words:

More Done

+

New Ideas

+

Less Time

+

More Fun

=

Synergy

This exercise takes only a few minutes to administer, but you should spend some time explaining the outcome to participants and how it relates to the work you're trying to accomplish organizationally. Perceptive people will understand why management is interested in teamwork: it increases productivity, creates new ideas, and saves time. But you also want them to realize there is a big payoff to employees: teamwork is more fun than the traditional work approach. Teamwork, when it works, not only wins people's heads, it wins their hearts.

A Clarification of Terms

The world of "bizspeak" has long been filled with vague and sometimes conflicting terminology, so to prevent confusion, let me clarify my terms.

I've just provided you with a definition of team. Lately, businesspeople have been prefacing the word "team" with adjectives that, in my opinion, change the meaning. For instance, I don't believe the term "self-managed team" is interchangeable with "self-directed team" (although some management writers seem to think it is). Self-managed teams take direction from a management team within the organization, but are responsible for determining how they will best fulfill expectations of them. They are not totally autonomous.

Conversely, self-directed teams are the most highly evolved form of teamwork. They operate independently. Rather than taking cues, they determine not only the "how" but the "what" of their efforts and let management know what they've decided. The self-directed team is a rarity. Despite the trend toward decentralized decision making and more participative employee involvement, I believe self-directed teams will be far less common than self-managed teams.

That's why I'll be addressing self-managed teams for the balance of this book. Some of these concepts can be applied to creating self-directed teams, but let's not get ahead of ourselves.

THE TEN CRITICAL DIFFERENCES BETWEEN A TEAM AND A WORK GROUP

Businesspeople use the word "team" loosely, but there are some substantive differences between a group and a team. Over the past six years, I've spent a great deal of time working with clients in hands-on organizational teambuilding. Having studied successful teams and talked with team leaders and members, I've identified 10 critical differences between a work group and a synergistic team.

Think about your people and use the following guidelines to determine whether you have a traditional work group or a highly functioning team.

Which Way Is Competition Directed?

The first question you need to answer is, "Who do your people compete against?" Here's one place where a sports analogy works. Whenever a professional team takes the field, it always has a clearly identified external opponent. Team members aren't competing against each other.

I mentioned earlier that optimal productivity not only doesn't require competition, sometimes it requires an absence of competition. There's an important difference between appropriate and inappropriate competition. Appropriate competition is directed outward; inappropriate competition is directed inward.

Work groups compete inward. Synergistic teams
compete outward.

Sometimes management pits manufacturing shifts against each other: the shift that produces the most by the end of the contest wins some kind of bonus. Sometimes one shift gets so far ahead so quickly that the others adopt a "we'll never catch up" attitude, and overall *performance actually decreases.*

Similarly, sales contests are often an example of destructive inner competition. There are always a few salespeople who know they don't have a chance of winning, so the contest doesn't motivate them at all. Sometimes such contests prompt a cutthroat sales rep to start sneaking business from other salespeople's accounts—and maybe even sabotaging their efforts. The result: You'll have a top producer at the end of the contest, but compare cumulative results of the group to a non-sales period, and you might be unpleasantly surprised.

Both of the previous situations could be improved by slightly changing the focus. In the manufacturing case, the contest would work like this: at the end of the month, any shift that has exceeded quota by 30 percent will win. Now shifts are focused on competing against a goal, rather than each other.

In the sales contest, inform your team that every 10 percent increase in business will result in a bonus for each team member. If the group can double sales, you'll treat them to dinner and drinks at their favorite bistro. Now, not only do the salespeople compete against a common goal, they cooperate to achieve it.

There are basically three things to compete against: *a competitor in the marketplace, a goal to be achieved,* or *a common problem to be solved.* Continually monitor which way competition is directed and focus team efforts outward.

Whose Agenda?

Teams operate from a shared agenda. Work groups usually operate from individual agendas.

Two characteristics a team must have are wisdom and discipline. *Wisdom is the ability to discern between the significant and the trivial.* Just as a wise individual knows what is most important to his personal success, a wise team knows what is most important to the team's success. There is a shared understanding of priorities and values. *Discipline is the ability to do what's important whether you want to or not.* It isn't enough to know what is important— even a traditional work group has some sense of priorities. But in a work group, ease of completion often determines when and how things get done. In a synergistic team, relative importance to the overall success of the team determines when and how well things get done.

In this context, an agenda becomes the focused effort to accomplish what is important to the team. Individual agendas rank second when team members are clear on what needs to be done if the team is to succeed.

Another practical benefit of a shared agenda: it gives team members the big picture—how their individual activities contribute to the larger whole. It's the difference being goal focused and task focused. In a work group, people sometimes do their jobs without any consideration of how their work affects the productivity of others. (We've all been on the receiving end of a job where the person doing it obviously didn't know, or care, how difficult it would be for the next person to pick up where they left off.) Team members learn to ask themselves two questions to avoid this:

- How will what I'm doing affect the next person in the process?
- How will it affect the final result?

A team agenda also helps team members prioritize. Teams know the critical difference between *efficient* and *effective.* Efficient is doing things right; effective is doing the right things. Work groups, lacking a team agenda, are often neither. Successful teams are usually both.

How well you do something matters little if you're doing the wrong thing. Here's a personal story you can use to illustrate this point with your team.

I was a very poor basketball player in junior high. But in the two minutes of court time I actually played, I managed to steal the ball from the other team. I can still remember the adrenaline surge as I drove down the court. To my amazement, no one was anywhere near me as I scored the single most perfect layup in my basketball career. When I turned around, the audience was on its feet. But they weren't cheering—they were booing and hissing. You've probably already figured out why: in my excitement, I had gone the wrong direction and scored a basket for the other team. I didn't realize it at the time, but I had just experienced the critical difference between being efficient and being effective. I had done the wrong thing very well.

To be successful, team members must understand three things. First, they need to know how their individual efforts contribute to the team's success; secondly, how what they're doing contributes to the success of other team members; and thirdly, how what the team is doing contributes to the success of the organization. Personal agendas are allowed only when they don't negate or contradict the team agenda.

Innovate or Evaporate

The third difference between a work group and a high performance team is that work groups are staid and stodgy. *Fortune* magazine once did an article on "killer competitor" companies that dominated their particular industries. *Fortune* found that most of these companies lived by the slogan, "innovate or evaporate." They were continually pursuing new ideas and processes.

High performance teams tend to be innovative—by necessity. Ohio State University football coach Woody Hayes used to say, "You're either getting better or you're getting worse." In a competitive world, status quo is a myth. Even if we manage to stay the same, the people and organizations around us continue to improve, so in a sense, we lose ground.

> *Good enough is never good enough, if better is possible.*

We must continually challenge ourselves to improve every aspect of how we do business. Work groups are content with the status quo, but pursuing and sharing new ideas must be high on the team's agenda.

Teams Don't Tolerate Tyrants

The fourth key difference between work groups and high performance teams deals with how decisions are made and implemented. Work groups are run in an autocratic manner: somebody decides and everybody else does. High performance teams operate participatively—the people who "do" also decide.

> *The cost of commitment is involvement.*

This is a commonly misunderstood concept. Involvement doesn't mean "management by committee." There are two primary reasons why this is not the case. First, team members don't need to be involved in every decision, nor do they want to be. Before putting a decision to the team, ask yourself a simple question: "Will they really care?" There are many instances when a directive decision-making style is convenient and expedient.

Secondly, there are times when the needs of the larger organization rule. One critical job of leadership is to assess the organizational environment, set direction, and decide what needs to be done. In these instances, involvement becomes critical after the decision is made. If management wants commitment, team members should be given an opportunity to decide how best to do what needs to be done. The average team member likes some sense of direction; what they resent is having absolutely no say in important decisions that affect them.

The only thing worse than not involving employees in the decision-making process is asking them to get involved, then expecting them to tell you what you want to hear.

If you can't live with the answer, don't ask the question.

What Kind of Starters?

Highly functioning teams are composed of self-starters. Work groups are composed of "kick-starters." Kick-starters do just enough to get by and frequently say, "They don't pay me enough to do that . . ." Kick-starters are not motivated by the hope of gain, but by the fear of loss. They do what's necessary so they won't lose their jobs or the next pay increase.

By comparison, self-starters are people who like to run a fast race. Self-starters are usually recruited, not made. The key is to look for team members who are self-motivated and then create a system that provides them with both external and internal rewards. (You'll find more about motivation in Chapter 10.)

Here are 10 words you can use to quickly determine whether you're dealing with a kick-starter or a self-starter. Before offering someone a spot on your team, tell them, "If you don't like to sweat, don't take this job."

Is There Linkage?

Linkage between team success and organizational success is a prerequisite for teambuilding. In a work group, what matters most is "my performance"—little consideration is given to the team's overall performance. A team is interested in the linkage between the success of the individuals and the team. But the likelihood of teamwork is small if people are rewarded and recognized only on the basis of individual performance. So the critical question you must answer:

What do team members enjoy when the team wins?

When a football team makes it to the Super Bowl, everybody on the team gets a Super Bowl ring. There is a direct payoff for being on a team that plays in the Super Bowl, and an even bigger payoff if the team wins. Recognition of individual performance is not eliminated, it is enhanced. Players are conscious that there is a bigger goal than simply playing well themselves. They understand the linkage between individual performance and team performance.

The highly successful Domino's Pizza uses a technique called TIPO, which stands for "team and individual performance objectives." Each month, managers sit down with employees and involve them in setting goals for themselves. But they don't stop there. Management clarifies team goals for the month. At the end of the month, if the team goals are met, there is a direct payoff to every team member. If team goals aren't achieved, everybody shares in the consequences. Within the TIPO system, people have responsibility for their own success as well as how they contribute to the team's success. Winning takes place on two fronts: individually and collectively.

Healthy Dependency

In a work group, people tend to be either independent or over-dependent. In a high performance team, people are interdependent.

Here's the difference. Overdependent people seldom get anything done without help from others. Independent people want to be left alone to do their jobs without assistance or feedback from others. Somewhere between overdependence and independence is a healthier zone of interdependency.

Interdependency is shared dependency that comes from under-standing that what we do affects others and vice versa. Interdependent people are willing to do two things: they ask for help when they need it, and they offer assistance when they can.

Pity the team leader who says, "Mark isn't a team player, but I'd hate to get rid of him because he does such a good job." One of the most devastating effects on any team is a colleague who has earned the right not to participate. That person is independent—and despite the results he may individually produce, often the effect on team morale is negative enough to offset any gains from his performance.

Touchy-Feely Stuff

Getting along with each other isn't a particularly lofty goal, but most groups are content with that. In a work group, people tolerate each other and they tolerate what they do for a living. Teams achieve more than tolerance. In a team, people enjoy their work and they enjoy who they do it with.

At your organization, does somebody greet you every morning with an "emotional raincoat"? An emotional raincoat is an un-spoken message that we shouldn't have too much fun. After all, work is serious, and to do it right, people need to suffer a little. But if we want to create high performance teams, it must be OK to work and have fun at the same time.

A Sense of Urgency

Work groups are plagued by Parkinson's Law, which states that work expands to fill the time allotted.

> *If you work in an organization where there are few significant deadlines, you're probably not achieving anything significant.*

A sense of urgency spurs performance. Think about the last time an edict came down on Friday afternoon that a major project had to be finished and shipped by Monday. You may have found that you were able to kick out over a weekend work that normally would have taken a month to produce.

We know both intuitively and quantitatively that few organizations are working at full potential. Urgency makes people accountable for producing results on time.

Thriving on Challenge

While work groups resist challenge, teams seem to thrive on it. Work groups avoid risk.

> *It takes a willingness to live with failure for people to be willing to try new things.*

Teambuilt organizations reward people for trying new things, regardless of the outcome. They celebrate those who try and fail just as much as they celebrate those who try and win.

Just because teams thrive on challenge doesn't mean that they don't sometimes moan and groan. Any group of people, when faced with a new challenge, will often respond that way. But teams move quickly through the complaining phase and accept the realization that "it's another tough challenge, but we've handled them before and we'll handle them again." Teams may not always choose to be challenged, but they ultimately respond constructively. They've learned that complaining only wastes valuable time that could be spent addressing the challenge.

WHERE TEAMWORK COUNTS

There are four areas where teamwork works best.

The first, and most obvious, is with employees or coworkers. Any group with a common objective, whether an ongoing team or a project team, can benefit from teamwork.

Secondly, these concepts can be used with other departments and groups in your organization to create interdepartmental/interorganizational teamwork.

The third and fourth areas are less common, but I encourage you to try teamwork with your customers and vendors. It can be very important for your customers, and for your organization, to identify common interests. Recognizing our interdependence with those we serve in the marketplace raises the question, "How can mutually beneficial results be achieved both for customers and for the people who are providing the goods and services they buy?"

Even more radical is the idea that teamwork can work with vendors. Often our relationships with vendors are competitive and adversarial. But why not treat vendors as allies? Improving these relationships will increase your likelihood of getting better terms, better treatment, better quality, and faster service.

Combining all four areas results in *input–output teamwork:* managing the input side of your business by building teams with your vendors, managing the teams of people who produce your products and services, and managing the output side of your business by building teams with your customers. Teambuilt organizations enjoy synergy in all these areas.

GETTING STARTED

Getting teamwork to work for you is really quite simple—but "simple" doesn't necessarily mean "easy." Here's one approach for converting your organization to the high performance teamwork concept. ***Assess Your Current Situation.*** Evaluate it on the basis of the 10 differences between teams and work groups. Each characteristic is listed here on a scale of 1 to 10; 1 represents the most extreme work group example, and 10 the extreme team example. You, the team leader, begin by scoring on the basis of where on the scale your group falls for each characteristic. Then give each team member this evaluation. Ask them to share not only their scores for each of the 10 characteristics, but the reasons why they chose those scores. The scoring is relative; specific suggestions for improvement will come from team members' explanations rather than the scores themselves.

Work Group	*Team*
competes inward	competes outward
personal agendas	team agenda
staid	innovative
autocratic	participative
kick-starters	self-starters
no linkage	linkage to team success
independent or overdependent	interdependent
tolerate each other	enjoy each other
little or no urgency	sense of urgency
resist challenge	respond to challenge

1 ◄—— 2 —— 3 —— 4 —— 5 —— 6 —— 7 —— 8 —— 9 ——► 10

This evaluation should help determine whether you're becoming teambuilt or still primarily in the work group mode.

Start Studying Other Successful Teams. Look at successful teams both within your industry and outside. Do a database search or other research to find articles and publications that will provide you real-world role models.

Once You've Targeted Some Role Models, Involve All the People Who Will Be Affected. When GM's Cadillac engine plant in Lavonia, Michigan, decided to go to a team concept, they pulled together a group of union officials, management, and hourly employees. That representative group studied other successful teams for over a year before putting together their own operating philosophy.

Solicit Concerns from Everyone. Recently I did some training for a large pharmaceutical company in the Midwest that's making a radical change to team-based manufacturing. One of the things we found very helpful was not only soliciting concerns from employees one-on-one, but also making anonymous questionnaires available.

You'll want to know what people are really concerned about, so make it easy for them to be totally candid. In your effort to solicit concerns, include these two open-ended statements:

"In my opinion, the biggest barrier to teamwork is _____."
"My misgivings about teamwork are _____."

Create a Timeline. Make sure your timeline is realistic—false starts can be devastating. You'll probably see some positive things happen quickly, within a matter of months, but a lasting shift to teamwork will take about two years. You're building for current and future success, so be patient. Make sure your timeline includes some milestones so people will know what's going to happen and when.

Inform and Train. As I already mentioned, teamwork does not come naturally to most of us. So you must provide everyone who will be involved with the basic training they need to start functioning as a team.

Start Small and Build. One of my largest clients has two manufacturing plants. At their plant on the West Coast, a supervisor got so turned on by reading a management book about teamwork that he went to the plant manager and said, "I think we can eliminate an entire level of management if you'll let us go to self-managed teams." The plant manager, a very wise and prudent man, said, "Why don't you try that with your guys first and see how it works out?"

A few months later, the supervisor's efforts had worked so well with his small group of eight that teamwork was rolled out to the rest of the department. Six months later, the teamwork concept was expanded to the rest of that California facility. And within 18 months, the company had started the same process at its headquarters. This is a good example of a reasonable rollout. Start small and build until you've got some proof that your approach will work.

Evaluate and Adjust. Don't fall so madly in love with the idea of teamwork that you become overcommitted. There are undoubtedly environments where teamwork, as it is presented here, may not work. One of the philosophies that have helped guide me in my own business:

What works, works.

Don't be afraid to change or modify your approach if what you've attempted hasn't given you the payoffs you expected. Also, don't be confined by the role models you choose, particularly if their circumstances are much different from yours. Instead, measure the success of your teambuilding by how current performance compares to pre-teamwork performance. Look at whether teamwork has created synergy and improved morale and bottom-line performance.

In the chapters that follow, I'll give you the six steps you need to create a *teambuilt* organization and make teamwork work.

3

STEP 1: LOCATE

*"Eagles don't flock, you've got to find
them one at a time."*
Ross Perot

There are only two ways to get talent: recruit it or develop it. It pays to do both. But it is much easier to develop talent when you begin with good potential. One of the most overlooked areas in corporate America today is the recruitment process. We don't get the people we need because we fall into any number of traps that prevent us from locating the potential we could eventually develop into talent.

Here are seven of the most common traps we face in locating any team member and some practical solutions for each.

Trap #1: "It's Tough to Teach a Dog Horse Tricks"

You've probably heard the saying, "It's tough to teach an old dog new tricks." Well, it's even tougher to teach a dog the tricks that horses are supposed to do. If you have a team of thoroughbreds, you need to hire potential thoroughbreds. But if you take whomever personnel sends you, you might end up with a dog. (If you do have a personnel department, remember that their job is to assist you, not decide for you.) Unfortunately, many team leaders take a hands-off approach to hiring.

You may already have a "dog" on your team—a nonperformer who just can't run the same race the rest of the team is running. When I hear managers complaining about these noncontributing team players, I usually ask two questions. First, "Who hired them?" And secondly, "If you didn't hire them, why are you letting them stay?" As a team leader, you must be actively involved in selecting the people you want on your team. Otherwise, you end up living with poor choices, or having to get rid of someone else's hiring mistake.

So where do "thoroughbreds" come from? You can always recruit them from within your organization; the downside to that is you might steal an excellent team player away from another team. Your gain is their loss. Sometimes it pays to rotate team members (I'll talk about job trading later), but you need to be sensitive to creating unhealthy internal competition to get the best team members.

There are some alternative sources for finding good team members outside your organization. By alternative, I don't mean running an ad in the classifieds or your trade publication, but recruiting through resources that aren't traditionally used. Here are a few pointers.

Heart-Hunters. Perhaps the single best way to find good people is through networking. This is a technique used by executive head-hunters, who are pros at recruitment and placement. They get paid to locate good people. But if you can't afford to turn over all your recruiting needs to an executive search firm, try heart-hunters instead—they don't cost anything.

A heart-hunter is anyone who knows your needs well enough to point you toward good people they know. This could include friends, business colleagues, customers, or even vendors. The key is to put the word out to your network of heart-hunters so they'll keep their eyes open for the kind of people you want and send them your way.

The School Tool. The second alternative source comes from establishing relationships with high schools and colleges. Many high schools and colleges look to the business community for resources such as guest speakers or advisory board members. Becoming such a resource is not just an altruistic gesture—it's a self-serving technique for connecting with some of the best talent coming out of high school and college classes today. Becoming a regular resource provides a tremendous opportunity to develop relationships with teachers and people in the educational system who can channel their best students to you before the formal recruitment process begins. By building relationships in advance, you're in the best position to skim off some of the top talent.

The Gray Market. The fastest-growing demographic group in America today is people aged 55 and older. Many of these people are motivated differently than younger employees. Their families are grown, they have a decent retirement income, but they're not ready to quit working. They come back into the work force not to earn a living, but to put meaning back into their lives, to feel like they're contributing. Walmart's "store greeters" are often members of this demographic group.

Trap #2: Nice Suit, but Don't You Have Three Just Like It?

Hiring is a little like shopping for clothes. Let's say you examine your wardrobe and decide that what you need is a gray pinstripe suit. You decide to visit a clothing store, where you look at a number of gray suits. But then you notice a nice blue suit on sale. It fits perfectly, and the next thing you know, you buy it. You feel good about your purchase—until you get home and put it in the closet, alongside the other three blue suits you already have.

You've just made a decision on the basis of want rather than need. We tend to do the same thing when we hire new employees.

Research shows that we often hire people we perceive to be like us. And if we're not careful, we end up in an environment we want to avoid—"the clone team." The point is to recruit on the basis of need. Identify in advance the kinds of skills and abilities needed to complement current team members. Determining what you need in advance will keep you from ending up with a bunch of blue suits and still missing that gray suit that's so important to your team's success.

Trap #3: Choosing from the Best of a Mediocre Bunch

I once saw a cartoon of a seedy politician holding a campaign sign that said, "Vote for Me—the Best of a Mediocre Bunch." Just as there is some truth in the humor of not having much choice at election time, we often don't have much to choose from when we hire a new team member. One reason is that we spend more time doing paperwork than looking hard for job candidates. The average manager just doesn't devote sufficient time to the task.

Some of the soundest business advice on recruiting comes from Harvey Mackay, who wrote the best-selling book *Swim With the Sharks Without Being Eaten Alive.* Mackay has been in the envelope business in Minneapolis for more than 27 years. More importantly, he says he has been open for hiring 52 weeks a year for all that time. If somebody solid comes through the front door, Mackay's got a job—even if he wasn't advertising a position. The strength of Mackay's recruiting efforts is reputation coupled with a continuous search for good talent.

Taking a chapter from Mackay's book, start your recruiting process now. And you should be recruiting continuously. If you don't, someday a key team member is going to give you two weeks' notice and you're not going to have much longer than that to replace him. If you haven't got some candidates identified and waiting in the wings, you'll be forced to choose from a mediocre bunch you were able to come up with on short notice.

Only Experts Need Apply

It's a familiar dilemma: a young person goes to an organization and asks for a job. The potential employer asks, "Got any experience?" The kid says no, so the employer isn't interested. Four years later the kid comes back to that same organization and applies again. Now, he explains he has four years experience. Still, he doesn't get the job. Why? Because now he's overqualified.

It seems we often want people with experience and expertise— just not too much. I know sales managers who like to hire people with no sales experience. That way, they don't have any preconceived notions or bad habits when it comes to selling. Lacking experience, they can readily be taught to sell effectively.

Sometimes the most difficult people to teach to be team players are those with many years of experience in a traditional work group environment. They may have learned to be very independent (remember, we haven't always recognized interdependence as a positive trait) and possess many ingrained habits that make it difficult for them to cooperate at all the levels necessary for team success. In a positive sense, someone with little or no experience is malleable and willing to learn.

Of course, experience does count for something (depending on the experience). But maybe the best experience is different experience. If you hire only people who posses basically the same expertise, you might end up with depth, but you'll lack diversity on your team.

My college degree is in agricultural economics, but I've also got some coursework in animal science. Many of the things I learned in ag school apply to business. Here's one: if you crossbreed livestock, you end up with something called *hybrid vigor*—the best traits of each parent. This oversimplified explanation is an apt analogy for teamwork. When you're recruiting, if you look for people with backgrounds and experiences different from those of existing team members, you can achieve a kind of hybrid vigor. The skills and knowledge of the team are enhanced by diversity and you end up with a team that benefits from the best that each team member possesses.

For example, if you're in a marketing team, it might not strengthen your team to hire another marketing expert. Maybe it would be more valuable to get someone from manufacturing, or somebody with a direct sales background. They could challenge your thinking and bring another perspective to the table. Hiring someone from a different industry also could bring to your team new ideas that were previously unconsidered.

There's nothing inherently wrong in hiring experts, but there is a lot to be gained by building a team of people with wide-ranging expertise.

Hiring "ACES" for Your Team

When it comes to recruiting and hiring for any group, here's an important maxim to keep in mind:

> *Hire team members who possess traits not easily taught.*

There are at least four traits that are difficult to develop in people, and they form the acronym ACES. When locating team members, you should be looking for "ACES."

Attitude. Stu Leonard runs a world-famous dairy store in Norwalk, Connecticut. This store sells 10 times more per square foot than the average grocery store in America. One reason is their incredible customer service. Incredible customer service is based on incredibly good employees. Leonard's employees are well-trained, but the process starts with hiring good people. Leonard says he doesn't care if potential employees understand the grocery business, what's most important is their attitude. Because if they have the right attitude, Leonard's can teach them about groceries. Only one out of every 25 applicants is accepted at Stu Leonard's, where they hire on the basis of attitude rather than expertise.

Cooperation. It is much easier to determine if somebody is a star performer than to tell if they're a team player. A résumé and history of accomplishments tells you only what a job candidate has achieved, not how it was achieved. One way to gain insight into someone's team potential is to ask a job candidate his greatest career accomplishment and how he did it. Then listen carefully for one word that ideally will be used often: "we." Giving credit to others is an indicator of cooperation. You don't want to recruit people who suffer from "superperson syndrome" and don't recognize or utilize the support and contributions of others. Few great things are accomplished without the involvement of many, and good team players take pride not just in what they've accomplished, but in what the group achieved.

Energy. Carl Sewell, of Sewell Cadillac in Dallas, Texas, is one of the most successful automobile dealers in America. Like Leonard's, Sewell Cadillac is a leader in volume and quality. Sewell looks for another important trait in potential employees: energy. He likes people who have a difficult time sitting still during job interviews because they'd rather be out doing something. Energy is a characteristic that clearly would be difficult, if not impossible, to instill through on-the-job training. Before inviting someone to join your team, consider how much drive they possess.

Service. The last several years have brought a flood of books and seminars on customer service. The problem with customer service is that the emphasis is on the word "customer" instead of "service." But service is created from the inside out. Providing exceptional service in the marketplace begins with serving internal customers: coworkers, employees, and other departments. To be effective, team members should understand that every job on the team provides a service to someone. They need to understand who their customer is, and how serving that customer contributes to the organization's overall success in the marketplace. Beware of those who focus on what they expect to gain from belonging to your team and look for those who have thoughtfully considered what they hope to contribute.

Trap #5: Style Over Substance

The fifth trap is flash over substance. Have you ever hired a charismatic flop or a personable dud? If you have, you understand how "flash" can distort the facts. Research shows that past performance is the single best indicator of future performance. Thus, an individual's accomplishments should receive more attention than his style.

Perhaps all the books and seminars on "how to get the job you really want" have unintentionally done us a disservice. Efforts to package job candidates seem to have made the packaging more important than the contents. I've heard of potential hires being eliminated because of a misspelled word in a cover letter. Granted, attention to detail is important, but is the correlation between spelling skill and teamwork truly significant?

I've met some pretty low-key people who were incredible team players. And I've met some terrific leaders who looked like they dressed for work in the dark. We need to balance our appraisals of potential team members so that we are looking at what will ultimately be important to the team's success. (Problems such as appearance are easier to deal with than a genuine lack of skill.)

One more bias that is dangerous in hiring: we tend to select people who are similar to us. This isn't always a conscious bias, but often we are drawn to job candidates who have similar education, background, and even style. Without really trying, you can create a team of clones—and lose the diversity that helps make teamwork work.

Trap #6: The Almost Oldest Vice

Trap six is an old vice: laziness. Early in my business career I had a boss who involved me in the hiring decisions for our team. I didn't actually decide who got hired, but I did provide input. One afternoon the receptionist phoned to tell me that my scheduled interview was coming up the elevator. Quickly shuffling through my in-basket, I found his résumé and read it—for the first time. I committed a terrible injustice to that interviewee, and to my team, by being so pitifully unprepared. Tragically, I don't think my lack of preparation was an exception. I've seen many others commit the same sin.

Hiring people is easy; hiring *good* people is tough work. And the toughest part isn't the interviewing—it's everything that precedes an interview. Laziness fosters a lack of effort to prepare, interview, and follow up.

Here are some basic steps you should take to prepare for a personal meeting with a team candidate.

1. Develop a specific profile of who you need, both in terms of skills and characteristics.

2. Tap traditional and alternative resources to identify potential candidates. The larger the pool of candidates you have to choose from, the better.

3. Obtain pertinent background information in addition to résumés. Study the résumé and prepare a list of interview questions. And check references. Few managers or team leaders take time to do this, and they often suffer later for this lack of effort.

    Here's a tip that may at first seem weird: If you can, get

the names and telephone numbers of three people the candidate would choose *not* to use as references. Candidates will be reluctant to provide this information unless you explain why. One positive reason to do this is that you may discover the very qualities which didn't make the candidate a great fit for another team will make him or her a perfect match for yours.

4. Schedule time with team members to meet and interview the person you're considering. If you don't, you'll fall prey to the next trap.

Trap #7: Even the Lone Ranger Asked Tonto for Advice

Hiring somebody to become a member of your team without exposing them to the other members is a grievous mistake.

I once lived in an apartment complex that used a marketing program called "pick your neighbor." Here's how it worked: If you recommended an apartment to someone and they moved in, you were paid $100. Plus, you had the added advantage of picking your neighbors. I was traveling 220 days a year then, and didn't really care who lived next door to me because I never saw them anyway. But the program started me thinking—wouldn't most employees love to have some input into who they work with eight hours a day? Call it the "pick your team members" program.

One of the biggest mistakes team leaders make is hiring a new employee without first getting input from team members. If you want to hire people who have not only the necessary skills, but the aptitude to work well with people already on the team, remember, involve as many team members as you can in the selection process. They will notice things you miss and provide insight in determining how well the team can work with the new hire. After all, who is better qualified to determine the "fit" of new team members than the people who will be working with them most?

The practice of team hiring took an unusual twist at a school near where I live. In June 1990, two 10-year-olds were recruited for a hiring committee interviewing candidates for principal of Cherry Creek Elementary School in southeast Denver. These students knew what they wanted: a principal who is "fun, not boring," who knows when to be "goofy" and when to be "serious," and who doesn't just sit in his office but is seen in classrooms, the lunchroom, and the playground talking with kids. Adults on the committee credited the fourth graders with insights that overcame a few teacher misgivings about letting students help pick the boss, according to a story in the *Denver Post.*

THE TEN-WORD STATEMENT TO MAKE *BEFORE* YOU MAKE THE OFFER

I know a retailer who spends the first 30 minutes of an interview trying to talk the job candidate into not taking the job. She says if a person is still interested in working there at the end of that 30 minutes, he or she must really love the business.

Sometimes in our enthusiasm for our team and organization, we run the risk of painting an overly optimistic picture. Weeks or months later, we end up with a team member who feels misled. I once had an interview with a potential employer who told me that nobody raised an eyebrow if you sometimes needed to come in late, leave early, or take a few hours of personal time. The reason, he said, was because there would be other times when I would need to work 12-hour days and on weekends. He concluded by saying that if I didn't like to run a fast race, I wouldn't enjoy working there.

Such candor is part of your job as team leader. So how can you make sure people will appreciate the commitment necessary to be a successful member of your team? Here are 10 words to say before you make a job offer: "If you don't like to sweat, don't take the job." It's much better to have an employee find out the job isn't as tough as he thought than be disappointed he's not enjoying a job of leisure.

Pay for a Day

Is there any way to "test" a potential team member? The owner of a Canadian landscaping company told me he pays a job candidate to work for one day. That way, both employer and potential employee have direct experience with each other and are in a better position to make an informed decision.

IDEAL TEAM SIZE

So how big should a team be? Big enough to get the job done. Seriously, there's no magic formula for calculating ideal team size. Traditionally, a range of 8 to 12 people has been widely recommended in management literature. But that's probably based more on old ideas about span of control than on optimum size for teambuilding.

Size can work against you if it cuts down on information flow or relationship development. At the same time, I have worked with teams of 80 that were more cohesive than teams of 8. Still, more often than not, the larger a team grows, the less effective it becomes. My suggestion:

Err toward smaller rather than larger.

When determining appropriate team size, focusing on *size* may be less useful than focusing on *symptoms*—because while you may never know if you're at optimal size, you'll certainly know when you're not.

Symptoms of a Team That Is Too Small

- the team has difficulty producing the results expected of it
- significant deadlines are missed
- team members work long hours and complain of overload
- details slip through the cracks
- the team frequently needs to go outside for expertise it lacks
- team members are involved in too many decisions they consider trivial

Symptoms of a Team That Is Too Large

- lack of camaraderie
- team members don't understand what other team members do
- low levels of personal interaction
- significant events or problems occur without all team members being aware
- team members feel uninformed
- information moves slowly
- decision making is either laborious or . . .
- . . . made without input from or regard for team members
- team members become territorial

Perhaps your team will be similar to what Alvin Toffler called "the pulsating organization" in his book *Powershift.* He defined a pulsating organization as one that expands and contracts in a regular rhythm and cites as an example the U.S. Census Bureau. Borrowing from this concept, many organizations might utilize "pulsating teams" that expand and contract on the basis of project or workload needs. Even in this context, the symptoms described will provide clues when the team is too small or too large.

4

STEP 2 : EDUCATE

Stanley Davis, in his powerful book *Future Perfect,* suggests holography as a potential model for leading organizations. A hologram is a
three-dimensional photograph created with lasers. The technology
is becoming very common. You may have seen holograms on credit
cards, in an amusement arcade, or even on inexpensive costume
jewelry. As Davis points out, holograms possess a unique property:
if the image is broken, any part of it will reconstruct the whole. That
is, each piece of the hologram contains the code for the whole.
Applying the holographic model to several aspects of business,
Davis asks, "Can it be said . . . for example, that the entire family
resides in each member, that the entire army resides in each soldier,
and that *the entire corporation resides in each employee?"*

I believe it is not only possible, but that, for teamwork to really
work, it must be so. The objective becomes creating a "holographic
team" so that the code for the team's success resides in every team
member. They must know, understand, and be committed to the
code for the team's success.

This raises three important questions for teambuilding:

1. What is the code for the team's success?
2. How do we make sure team members know and understand it?
3. How do we get people committed to it?

The answers:

1. The code includes the team's

    - vision
    - mission
    - values
    - goals
    - expectations

2. Educate
3. Motivate (the topic of Chapter 10)

COMPONENTS OF THE HOLOGRAPHIC TEAM

Business philosophers are sometimes characterized as people who don't know what they're talking about, but who make you feel responsible for not understanding. I don't want to be guilty of perpetuating unnecessary business jargon and rhetoric; my goal is to provide a pragmatic philosophy of teamwork. For example, I have heard the word "mission" defined several different ways and even used interchangeably with "vision." My goal is to clarify, in language everyone can understand, the meaning of each term I use to define the holographic team.

The Vision

In simplest terms, "vision" answers the question, "*Where* are we going as a team?" A team's vision is its view of the future. It gives people a destination to work toward.

Vision is probably one of the least understood concepts in organizational teambuilding today. Although the words "vision" and "mission" are often used interchangeably, in reality, they are very different. Proverbs 29:18 says, "Without a vision, the people will perish." Team members need a clear picture of where they're going and what the future will look like if the team is successful.

Likewise, good leaders know that without people, the organization's vision will perish. Teamwork requires both destination and transportation, that is, a worthwhile vision and people to help fulfill it.

An inspiring team vision involves these four components:

The Vision Must Be Desirable to All Involved. Many organizations have very nice vision statements that do not represent the needs of the people who work there. They are management's view of the future—not employees'. The vision statement needs to paint a picture of a future where everybody wants to work and do business—not just team leadership.

It Must Be Ambitious but Realistic. If you formulate a vision that is totally unachievable, it becomes nothing more than rhetoric—and rhetoric has no power to motivate people. Team members will generally respond well to challenge if the challenge is realistic. But an unrealistic view of the future discourages rather than motivates.

The Vision Should Give Reason to the Team's Daily Effort. As people go about their business every day, they should be able to see how the vision is moving them closer to where they want to be. The vision should create a sense of continuity and purpose in what is being done.

Leadership Has Got to Live the Vision. It doesn't do much good to preach customer service if your top managers haven't seen a real-life customer in the last two weeks because they're behind closed doors in high-level meetings. Team members don't take seriously managers who talk about a commitment to quality but have never visited, much less worked, a shift on the shop floor. For a vision to be effective, employees must see it demonstrated in the daily activities of leadership.

Here are some techniques you can use to develop a working vision for your team.

Project Forward in Time. Create in your mind a clear picture of what your team should look like in five years. As you call on your imagination, here are some questions to stimulate your thinking and help you define your team's future:

- What will be your team's role and importance within the organization?
- Will the team be larger? Smaller? Why?
- If the team's larger, where are those new team members going to come from?
- If it's smaller, where are the departing team members going to go?
- Five years from today, who will your customer be?
- How will you be serving them differently?
- What are you going to be producing, i.e., what will your team's primary products or services be?
- What levels of quality will you be providing with those products or services?
- How quickly will you be making it?

Consider the quality of work life for team members in five years:

- What are their perks and benefits going to be?
- What will their earnings potential be?
- What new education, training requirements, and opportunities will exist for team members?
- What will the work environment and facilities be like?

Find Out What's Important to Those You Serve and Support. Imagine that you are interviewing two other departments you interact with organizationally. If you were to ask them what two things they like most about your team, what would you want them to say? This will help you to answer the question, "As a team, what do we want to contribute to other teams, and be appreciated for?" (To find out how much the team needs to do to achieve this vision, actually ask two other departments what two or three things they appreciate most about your team. Compare their answers to what you'd like them to say, and you now have an idea of your team's "success gap.")

Learn from a Team Mentor. Don't limit your mentor to sports teams: find an organization—private, nonprofit, or public sector—that you really respect. This mentor doesn't need to be perfect (you can learn from their mistakes as well as their successes), but they do need to typify the team concept. Study them by obtaining any printed material available. If possible, arrange to interview some of their leadership and team members to find out what has worked best for them and what important lessons they've learned. Perhaps someone from their team might be willing to serve as an informal consultant and provide you with feedback about your teambuilding attempts.

Write Your Team's Success Story. Get a magazine cover from *Forbes, Fortune,* or maybe your favorite trade publication. Take a photo of your team, impose it on the cover, and then write the article you would like to see in that magazine someday. Be sure to convert your goals and aspirations to present tense: write about what your team has accomplished, the numbers they're producing, and the handicaps and obstacles that have been overcome. Then do some future-tense interviews and quote what team members will be saying about how the team has succeeded. This is a bit corny, but so what? There's nothing wrong with having a little fun and getting people to think at the same time. Post the magazine cover and accompanying article somewhere it can be seen and read by your team.

At Least Once a Year, Ask Team Members to Develop Their Personal Vision. This vision should include what they'd like to accomplish, skills they'd like to learn, the things they'd like to be doing, and the positions of responsibility or leadership they'd like to have someday. After they've jotted down their ideas, schedule a breakfast or lunch to sit down with them to discuss what they've come up with. This exercise keeps you in touch with their personal values and goals. It can also help you, as team leader, determine in advance any potential conflicts between what your team members need to be happy and what you're actually going to be able to provide.

Testing for Practicality

After you've formulated your team vision, periodically test to see if people understand the vision and are receiving value from it. Here are four questions you can ask:

1. *"Do You Know What Our Team Vision Is?"* Ask everyone that question to find out if all hold the same vision for the future.

2. *"Were You Involved in Creating the Vision?"* In other words, does it represent what members feel the future should look like?

3. *"Is Our Vision of the Future a Place That You Personally Want to Do Business In?"* Maybe you're heading in a direction that precludes the participation of some team members who are currently

happy, but maybe won't be in the new world that awaits you down the road.

4. "Does Our Vision Help You in Day-to-Day Decision Making and Goal Setting?" If people can answer affirmatively to this and the other three questions, you'll know you have a vision that's more than rhetoric—you have a vision that gives people practical guidance and direction, and empowers them to accomplish the work of the team.

The Mission

Peter Drucker is considered by many to be the father of modern business management. Drucker says, "To make a living is no longer enough. Work also has to make a life."

People are increasingly concerned with not only how much money they make, but how they make their living. As I'll explain later, I believe the equation for motivating team members in the '90s will be:

$$Motivation = Money + Meaning$$

An organization's mission gives people a sense of purpose. Team members understand what they do and have a reason for doing it. The why is as important as the what. The mission answers the question, "Why?"

Several years ago my friend Darby Checketts, author of *Baseball, Bouillabaisse, and The Best of Class,* was researching a book on why people take pride in their work. He spent several summer months traveling with his son though the Midwest, interviewing people at random. While driving through one small rural community, they were attracted to the large sign on the firehouse lawn. Below the name of the fire department was this inscription: *"We Proudly Make the Difference."* Checketts thought this would be a great place to do an interview.

He went inside, approached one of the firefighters on duty, and explained the book project he was working on. He asked to talk to someone about the sign, "We Proudly Make the Difference." The firefighter looked at him and said, "Then you better talk to the sign painter."

So much for catchy slogans. Somebody in city government—maybe the fire chief—must have decided that their fire department needed a mission, something firefighters could rally around. The problem was, nobody checked with the firefighters to see if they really wanted to "proudly make the difference." My hunch is that many an organizational mission statement suffers the same rhetorical fate. The average team member probably doesn't know, or care, what the mission statement is, wasn't involved in creating it, and therefore, isn't committed to it.

Developing a Practical Mission

The essence of any practical mission should reflect the core purpose of the team. It should answer the question, "What is the team's purpose?" An organizational mission statement explains why the organization exists in the marketplace. Since most teams are part of a larger organization, the team's mission must complement and be compatible with the organizational mission statement. The team's mission might include the words ". . . to support and assist others in XYZ Company in becoming the leading supplier of . . ." It is important that the team's mission not be isolated or disjointed from the organization's larger purpose.

Secondly, to be effective, a mission should be challenging and exciting. As you'll soon read in the section on goals, people aspire to be better, if not the best, in their area. Challenge people with a mission worth committing to.

The mission should also reflect a sense of who the team serves. That may be customers in the marketplace, or another group or departments within your own organization.

Finally, a practical team mission should reflect input from team members. This prevents "The Firehouse Effect" I described in the previous story. Ask team members what they feel should be included in the mission—what is important to them and what can they commit to. Then try to represent as many of their ideas as feasible in the finished statement.

Federal Express has one of the finest mission statements in corporate America. Though it doesn't exactly follow the guidelines I've just given you, it works because it succinctly explains the business that Federal Express is about: *"People, service, profits."* These three words integrate the values and priorities shared by employees of the organization. Federal Express has found that if you take care of your employees, they will take care of their customers, and the profits will follow. (This effective mission statement could be the shortest business primer ever written.)

Here's a test for clarity: Can you write your team's mission on the back side of a business card? If you can't, it is too long. People won't be able to remember, and probably won't buy into, a mission that isn't focused and concise. Why not print the team's mission on the back of your business cards? That way, both team members and customers will know what you stand for. If your team members don't have business cards: *why not?* And don't say they're not needed. Important people have business cards. If your team doesn't, that's one little tip-off that they aren't "important." If people are proud of what they do and where they work, they deserve a small symbol of their organization's reciprocal pride. Business cards are such a symbol.

How can you make sure that the people on your team understand the mission? Ask them. Do a man-on-the-street survey. Ask somebody at lunch, "What is our mission . . . and what evidence do you have today that it makes sense?" Anybody can memorize a mission statement, but what you want is to hear them articulate the mission in their own words and capture the essense of what the team is about. To get people thinking about how that mission applies to everyday effort, ask them, "Who have you encountered today that typifies the team mission? What are you doing that demonstrates you believe in the mission?" A mission makes sense only if it is relevant. Asking team members these questions will keep them focused on why the team exists.

The Values

Vision is an explanation of where the team is going. Mission tells the team why they're going there. The purpose of values is to define the team's integrity and answer the question, "How will we get there?"

Historically, values haven't been a hot topic in business management. We've been more interested in results than in how we created the results. Yet the two are inextricably intertwined. One of the brightest business thinkers alive is Paul Hawkins. Maybe you've seen him on the PBS special, "Growing a Business," based on his book of the same title. Hawkins has said, "We must first *have* values before we can *add* value."

Merck & Co. has repeatedly been been voted "America's most admired company" in *Fortune* magazine's polls of CEOs. Studies conducted by Summit Consulting Group revealed five core values that are unanimously agreed upon from the CEO through first-level management, and across all divisions.

Values identify what is important to an organization. They tell people what beliefs and practices are held in highest regard and, thus, direct and guide the behavior of individuals within the organization. Without identified values, we end up with a preponderance of rules, policies, and procedures. Instead of communicating to people what's important, we tell people *what to do.* Often the result is team members who blindly follow the rules, even when it means doing things that don't make sense to them.

Would it be possible to live without rules, policies, or procedures? I'm not referring to state and federal laws imposed by our legislators, but the bureaucratic mess we create ourselves. In a rational world, we understand what is important. But in an attempt to communicate that to others, we create rules, policies, and procedures. And as the world around us changes, we create new rules and more policies and procedures to deal with the change. But we seldom stop to reevaluate the old rules to see if they still make sense. So before long, we've created a system where following the rules supersedes getting anything accomplished.

There is an alternative: *"Bend or Flex or Break the Rules, but Don't Ever Violate the Values (BOFOGA)."* Roy Disney once said, "When values are clear, decision making is easy." You can replace rules, policies, and procedures with judgment, but only if team members understand the values. That means you must be able to answer the question, "What are the values that drive our team?" Those values need to be consistent with your organization's values; more importantly, team members need to know what values to turn to when faced with a choice. Clearly identified values give people an opportunity to exercise their judgment.

Judgment Is Knowing When to Break the Rules. If you rely on team members to use their judgment, won't they sometimes make bad judgment calls? Of course they will. But then again, they make bad decisions even when they have a 357-page policy manual to refer to. The beauty of values is that employees will make better decisions more often and bad decisions more quickly. In our rapidly changing world, team members need to be able to act quickly. And they can't do that if they have to look up the answer before knowing what they should do. Judgment is the only logical choice.

BOFOGA . . . but don't violate the values.

The last two components of the holographic team are goals and expectations for both team members and the team leader. But we'll cover these in the next three chapters.

TRAINING FOR TEAMWORK

This chapter has focused on educating team members about the genetic code of the team's success. But it isn't enough for them to understand the *what* and *why* of teamwork; they need to learn the *how* as well. The word "education" comes from the Latin "educere," which means "to lead." Teambuilt organizations emphasize education, and that becomes a key ingredient in what makes them industry leaders.

As I've already said, teamwork isn't second nature to the people we work with. If the bad news is that most employees have never learned to cooperate with others to make teamwork work, the good news is that the important lessons of teamwork can be taught. Teamwork training requires a commitment of resources, both time and money.

Why does it seems that most organizations are more willing invest in *things* than in *people*? Even though the industrial age has given way to the information age, old habits and ways of doing business still linger: spend money on equipment that depreciates, and accounting treats it as a capital investment, but invest in employees, whose value appreciates with training, and it's called a "business expense." Savvy leaders know that the semantics of conventional accounting have not caught up to the realities of the workplace.

The New Competitive Edge

The buildings and equipment that your organization now utilizes your competitors could build or buy. Similarly, the technology you use your competitors could buy or develop themselves, and the capital you borrow or raise is available to them from the same fiduciary sources. When it comes to facilities, equipment, technology, and capital, there is little, if any, sustainable competitive advantage. Just as in computing, the software of a team is more valuable than the hardware. Both are necessary, but there's no question where the true value resides. In teamwork, soft knowledge is more valuable than hard assets. And if intellectual capital is the new competitive edge, then *education and training are the soundest investments.*

The new competitive edge is determined by your organizational commitment to develop the skills and competencies of every team member. Teambuilt organizations develop their edge by being committed to:

Learn more, learn better, learn faster

The following ideas form the foundation every organization needs for teaching—and learning—the important lessons of teamwork.

Begin by Developing a Teamwork Curriculum. The teamwork curriculum supplements job-specific training employees are (or should) already be receiving on an individual basis. Design your curriculum around two components, teamwork philosophy—the what and why—and teamwork practice—the how. The philosophy component should include, but not be limited to, the basics of the holographic team: vision, mission, values, goals, and expectations. Include your organization's history of involvement in and commitment to teamwork. Involve upper management in communicating corporate philosophy about teamwork and how they envision it working within your organization. Their involvement in early teamwork training will signal their commitment to the concept. One of the most powerful ways for them to do this is to participate in teamwork training as learners—and not just teachers. Upper management should be learning along with their team members, not independent of them, as is often the case.

The second component, the practice of teamwork, should include, at a minimum, these skills: interpersonal relationship skills, communication, cooperation, conflict resolution, group creativity/innovation, and problem solving.

There is great potential for overlap between skill sets, such as communication and interpersonal relationship skills. But you can avoid that through thoughtful planning. Remember to integrate existing training programs—personality styles, various quality and service programs, for example—with the teamwork curriculum so that no training appears "tacked on" as an afterthought.

Schedule Regular Team Training Sessions. As much as possible, the team should receive core training as a group. Training team members individually will be much less effective in developing camaraderie and group skills. Work with team leaders well in advance to schedule these training sessions so there can be few excuses for lack of participation. In those inevitable cases when team members miss a session, schedule them into the next available session. This assumes that team training is ongoing, as it should be, and not a one-shot event.

Your own department, group, or section can become teambuilt using these ideas, but it works best when there is an organizational commitment to make every department or group teambuilt. If training is sporadic or offered only to a few, you'll end up with isolated pockets of teamwork, and these teams will become frustrated by their inability to use a teambuilt approach when interacting with other groups or departments.

Getting your group to function as a team is tough. The only thing tougher is getting different groups in the same organization to work together.

Some groups have a natural antagonism toward other groups within their company. For instance, sales might think manufacturing is unresponsive to their customers' needs. But manufacturing might justifiably believe the sales team makes unreasonable demands. How, then, do you get the manufacturing team to cooperate with the sales team?

One answer is *team trading*. Begin by taking the person from sales who complains the most about manufacturing and put that person on the manufacturing team for a week. Then give the biggest moaner from the manufacturing team a chance to work in sales for a week. The essence of team trading is giving people the opportunity to work briefly as members of other teams they interact with.

Team trading provides several benefits. First, the price is right—it doesn't cost anything but time. Team members should work as part of a different team two to four times per year. Ideally, every team member will have some experience on every team. Remember, when someone is traded into a team for a short time, their primary purpose is to *learn* rather than *perform.*

Team trading creates empathy. You may not always agree with the other team, but firsthand experience with them will give you better insight into the challenges and dilemmas they face. Team members usually become more understanding, helpful, and patient once they've "played on the other team."

Finally, team trading stimulates critical thinking because the team tradee will ask lots of questions. Team members might falsely conclude that many of these questions are obvious or even dumb, but the proper perspective is that the questions are challenging—they cause team members to reexamine what they do and how they do it.

(One of the best ways to better understand what you do is to try explaining it to somebody who doesn't know.)

Anticipation Avoids Consternation

It is frustrating to be expected to do something long before you know how. For example, many of us go from a "doing job" into a management job with absolutely no management training whatsoever. You come into work one morning and they present you with your own office and some people and tell you "Good luck, Godspeed, and get results."

As someone who has given literally hundreds of management seminars, I can tell that a large percentage of people who attend are managers who have been managing for months, if not years, without benefit of any formal management training. Sure, most of them have been getting by and a few even seem to be naturals. But the situation still presents a paradox: Why don't managers get trained before they start managing?

Training people after they've already assumed new responsibilities is retroactive training. It is the cause of great consternation for people who want to do better but have never been taught how. The antidote is something I call "strategic anticipation."

Strategic anticipation means that career changes are anticipated and every increase in responsibility is preceded by the appropriate training and education. Again, this approach costs nothing because you'll eventually need to train them someday anyhow. Just do it before, not after, the fact. This is important not just for getting team members up to speed, but for teaching team leaders the types of leadership skills they'll need to expedite the team's success.

Serve Self-Paced Learners

Create a Corporate Resource Center That Can Be Utilized by All Teams Within Your Organization. Some team members will be motivated to learn beyond what is required. A corporate resource center is a lending library that enables individuals to take advantage of educational resources that might not otherwise be available. All you need to set up a resource center is a filing cabinet or credenza filled with the following:

- books
- magazines and trade publications
- audio cassette tapes
- video cassette tapes
- interactive software

Be Sure to Include Professional Development as a Part of Every Team Meeting. In Chapter 9, "Communicate," I'll explain the elements of effective team meetings. One of those elements is professional development in the form of audio or video presentations, team exercises, or guest speakers.

5

BEYOND GOAL SETTING

The building blocks of team success are goals. The term "goal set-ting" frequently is used to describe the process of formulating goals. As important as goal setting is, it is only part of the larger process of being goal-directed.

Success isn't about setting goals, it is about achieving them. Work groups focus on setting goals. Teams concentrate on achieving them.

Contrary to popular belief, goals are an overrated motivational tool. Giving people goals doesn't usually motivate them. I could pick a goal for you that I feel is very important or worthwhile, but if you don't have a reason for achieving that goal, you won't be motivated.

Three reasons why goals are ineffective:

- No reason to achieve them
- No excitement
- No commitment

To counteract that, leaders must:

- Provide a vision and mission—a reason why the goals are important
- Raise their team's sights by setting challenging goals
- Involve their team in goal setting and creating ownership

The most important function of goals is to *create accountability.* Goals give a team feedback on how much progress is being made and answer the question, "Are we getting closer to our vision?"

RAISE THE TEAM'S SIGHTS

Gen. H. Norman Schwarzkopf distinguished himself as a great leader during Operation Desert Storm. According to a story in *Inc.* magazine, early in his career he had been placed in charge of helicopter maintenance. When he asked how much of the helicopter unit was able to fly on any given day, he was told 75 percent. In tracking the performance of the unit, Schwarzkopf found that team members didn't come in at 74 percent or 76 percent, but always at 75 percent because ". . . that was the standard set for them." Schwarzkopf told *Inc.* he decided to raise the team's sights. "I said, 'I don't know anything about helicopter maintenance, but I'm establishing a new standard: 85 percent.' " Within a short time, the team had lived up to the new expectation and 85 percent of the helicopters were flying each day.

One of the greatest dangers any team faces is setting their goals too low. In 1984, Michael Dell launched a mail-order computer company in his University of Texas dorm room, using $1,000 in savings. Today Dell Computer is doing $679 million in sales and Dell, 26, is worth $282 million. "I don't believe in setting goals that are limiting," Dell says. "If you are going to set in place a strategy, it should be a strategy to lead."

Examine the goals of your own team. Do they represent a strategy of survival or of success? Mediocrity or excellence? One of the common denominators of high performance companies is a commitment to lofty goals. That's because team members don't get excited about being market also-rans; they want to be market leaders. This sage advice from the motto of city planners is still valid: "Make no little plans: they have no magic to stir men's blood."

GETTING PEOPLE TO OWN TEAM GOALS

Bear Bryant was the winningest coach in college football history. His teams won more than 323 games in the course of his career, thanks to his skill at getting players committed to the team's goals. Here's how he did it: At the beginning of each season, Bryant would ask all of the players to determine their personal goals for the coming season. Then he would sit down, go over every list, and incorporate as many of the players' personal goals into the team's goals as possible. In doing so, he communicated three very important messages: 1) I value you as an individual so I want to know what's important to you, 2) I want you to achieve your goals, 3) by combining team and individual goals, you know that *when the team wins, you win.*

The essence of great teamwork is linking individual and team success. This creates ownership. Because team members have a vested interest in their own success, they have an equal investment in the team's success.

CLARIFY THE TARGET

Team members can't hit a target they can't see. A properly formed goal vividly clarifies what needs to be accomplished. There are five aspects to an effective team goal:

- what
- how well
- how much
- by when
- for whom

The What

The "what" is usually obvious, but it should be examined for soundness by asking these questions:

- Will achievement of this goal move us closer to fulfilling our vision?
- Is it consistent with our sense of purpose?
- Who inside and outside the team needs to be involved in its achievement?
- Who is best suited to be involved? To lead?
- What priority should this goal take relative to the other important goals and tasks the team is involved with?

The How Well

Some things are worth getting done. Some things are worth doing well. Some things are worth doing very, very well. Perfectionism is the inability to tell the difference.

One of the greatest wastes of team resources is trying to do everything equally well. This occurs when team members lack a sense of priorities. Not every document needs to be presentation quality (especially if it's only used internally with the team). Not every task should be approached with the same intensity and scrutiny. Identify what level of quality is expected for each goal and task.

The How Much

Have you ever asked for a short report and received a book? Have you ever wanted a thorough analysis only to receive a short report? Another goal killer and waster of resources is a lack of quantification. "How much" relates to both quantity and thoroughness. It clarifies the amount of output expected.

The By When

Deadlines are necessary for planning. Vague requests such as "ASAP" have no meaning among team members — or between different teams—who work under different pressures and workloads. Team members need to know when they are expected to perform and complete their assignments if they are to have any sense of control.

The For Whom

Often overlooked is a sense of "Who are we doing this for?" Identifying the "customer" who will benefit from the completed goal, whether the customer is internal or external, one or many, has at least two benefits. First, it brings a sense of humanness to the activity. The director of a state agency in New York once told me that many of his staff considered themselves "paper pushers." "My job," he said, "is to show them that if they goof up the paperwork, they give a real human being somewhere an ulcer." Making team tasks more human raises the level of commitment.

Secondly, by knowing who they're doing something for, team members can factor in subtle changes that will improve the outcome of the project. Rather than acting to serve a generality, the team can target what things are most important to the specific customer.

THE RESULTS CALENDAR YEAR

Several years ago, some managers from Blue Cross/Blue Shield attended a teambuilding seminar I presented in Philadelphia. Months later I ran into one of these managers. She told me, "Of all the ideas you presented that day, the biggest leap in productivity for us came from your concept of *the results calendar year.*"

Every organization in America operates within a fiscal calendar year. Without one, the organization would not be able to meet deadlines necessary to keep it financially accountable. Without an accurate idea of its financial situation, planning becomes moot and measuring financial performance impossible for an organization.

A results calendar year serves the same purpose for teams, yet I know of few organizations that use them. A results calendar year is an accountability measure for making your team responsible for producing results on time and for achieving targeted goals quarter by quarter, over a 12-month period.

Consider this: You and your team members probably joined your organization long after it was started. Realistically, most of you will be gone (working at a different company, retired, etc.) long before your organization is gone. This creates a subconscious conspiracy:

Since the organization will outlast the team, you and
your team members are in no big hurry!

In the typical organization, the unconscious conspiracy lulls people into a state of short-term, day-to-day deadlines. Since there is little sense of urgency, few significant long-term goals are accomplished. The results calendar year counteracts this phenomenon.

At the end of each calendar year, meet with your team for the express purpose of picking 5 to 10 significant things the group agrees it can and should accomplish in the coming year. You know what performance management expects and demands of the team. The results calendar year identifies goals *above and beyond what is necessary.* Doing what is required maintains the status quo; true progress comes from doing what hasn't been done before.

Allocate time and, if necessary, financial resources that will be needed quarter by quarter. Determine a timeline and commit to tracking compliance or deviance. Although these team goals aren't required by management, don't pursue them if you aren't completely committed. Otherwise, you'll end up doing yet another futile exercise in planning that nobody takes seriously.

THERE'S MORE THAN ONE WAY TO SET A GOAL

We've established that teambuilt organizations use goals to create accountability. The goals the team establishes for itself or is asked to achieve by management provide a sense of whether progress is being made toward the team vision. In Chapter 8, I'll explain a cooperative activity for strategizing goal achievement, but at this point, I want to share the types of goals that teams can pursue.

The types of goals that a team pursues determines the types of results it achieves. High performance teams should use a mix of at least five different types of goals. Before you read further, write down the three to five most important goals your team is currently working on. (If you were to ask other team members to do this, would they write down the same goals?) As I explain each of the following goal types, decide which category each of yours falls into.

Improvement Goals Focus the Team on Doing Better. The primary benefit of improvement goals is that they prevent complacency— the No. 1 killer of teambuilt excellence. If your team has been successful for a long time, members may have settled into a comfortable mode where they're no longer pushing the envelope.

The greatest danger a team faces isn't that it won't become successful, but that it will, and then cease to improve.

An improvement goal is met whenever you exceed current levels of performance. Some examples: reducing costs, increasing production or sales, speeding up customer response time, and improving quality or service. Even failing less often is an improvement goal. If your team is currently behind in performance, one improvement goal could be to move closer to that performance standard.

A familiar management adage is that you can't improve what you can't measure. That's not really true. You can improve what you can't measure, but you won't know that you've improved. Improvement goals must give the team tangible feedback on how it is doing. But to accomplish that, the team must first be able to measure current levels of performance. Because this is usually hard work, it isn't often done. Find some standard of performance—even if it is imprecise—to benchmark future performance. That way, improvement goals can become part of your team agenda.

Fixed Target Goals Are the Most Familiar Type. These goals are usually defined in numerical terms. The achievement of a fixed target goal occurs when that predetermined standard is met.

The problem with fixed target goals is that they can cap results. Take, for example, a goal to increase sales by 20 percent in a given month. Once the sales team has met the goal, they often quit trying to do better—even if there's still two weeks left in the month. The team might have been capable of increasing sales 35 percent that month, but because the goal was 20 percent, management and team members were content once they reached it. The way to avoid capped performance is to split fixed target goals into three categories: meets numbers, exceeds numbers, and far exceeds numbers.

Let's assume that your fixed target goal is $1 million in sales this month. Assessing the team's talent and current market situation, you, as team leader, believe this goal is realistic. The team is probably capable of more. Your objective is to get the team at least to $1 million, and beyond if possible.

The "meets numbers" goal is $1 million. There is no formula for "exceeds numbers" goals (obviously anything above $1 million counts), but the psychological key is to *make the exceeds numbers goal achievable enough to keep team members pushing*. Depending on your team's potential and the challenges of your marketplace, 10 percent to 25 percent above your meets numbers goal might be reasonable. For purposes of illustration, let's make your exceeds numbers goal $1.25 million—25 percent beyond the meets numbers target goal.

What really drives above-average goal achievement is linking an additional reward or bonus to meeting the exceeds numbers goals. For example, everybody gets a $250 bonus if the team meets numbers. But if they achieve exceeds numbers, there will be a huge party at the end of the month and a $500 cash bonus for each team member.

Don't forget to determine your "far exceeds numbers" goals. Maybe your team really surprises you. By the second week they've already sold $1.25 million and you don't want them to coast for the rest of the month. After figuring your profit margin on sales, you announce that if they sell $2 million by the end of the month, not only do they get the cash bonus and the party, but the party will be held on a wonderful Caribbean island during an expenses-paid trip for everybody. (Just make sure the far exceeds numbers goal enables you to afford whatever payoff you choose.)

Remember, unless you've set your meets numbers goal too low to begin with, *you will need a significant incentive to get people to put in the kind of work necessary to achieve a far exceeds numbers goal.* There is nothing wrong with announcing a far exceeds numbers goal when you're already into the goal achievement period. By waiting, you'll have additional information about what a reasonable far exceeds numbers goal should be and the team will be benefiting from the momentum of current success. (One of the most important principles of goal setting, whether for individuals or teams, is that the goal should be both challenging and achievable. A goal the team believes is unrealistic will not usually be attempted.)

Meets, exceeds, and far exceeds numbers goals are an effective tri-level system that prevents your fixed target goals from capping performance.

Consistent Challenge Goals Are Ones That Can Be Achieved but Are Difficult to Sustain. Examples include being No. 1 in your industry, holding dominant marketshare, being recognized as the most innovative company among your competitors, or having the best quality in your product category.

The purpose of a continuing challenge goal is to sustain drive and focus your team on how they are performing compared to the competition. This type of goal is another way to battle the complacency that threatens any successful team.

Consistent challenge goals are sometimes set by management and are almost always bigger than any one team's ability to achieve them. Therefore, this type of goal usually requires inter-departmental teamwork and creates camaraderie within the organization. These goals are effective in helping team members see how their accomplishments fit into the bigger scheme of overall success in your industry.

Moving Target Goals Are Aimed For, but Never Reached. They're idealistic. (You must be wondering what the purpose of an unachievable goal is.) This is the one exception to what I said earlier about an unrealistic goal seldom being attempted. The purpose of a moving target goal is to illustrate that:

*No matter how successful the team becomes, it can still
get better.*

A moving target goal keeps fire in the team's belly so that members
are always looking for better ways to do things.

Moving target goals often include adjectives such as "legendary"
and "unequaled," as in "legendary service" and "unequaled quality." In a competitive world, yesterday's unequaled quality can
become tomorrow's industry average. The team needs to be con-
stantly reminded that it is critically important to continuously pursue improvement and new levels of accomplishment. History has
repeatedly shown that what we once thought was impossible often
isn't. Moving target goals redefine future success.

***Higher Purpose Goals Are Larger than Team Members or the
Team Itself.*** These goals tie into a sense of purpose, such as serving
God, doing business in the most ethical manner, enriching the lives
of employees, preserving the environment, and addressing injustice
in the community or society at large. The Tattered Cover Book Store
in Denver has set as one of its higher purpose goals playing an active
role in maintaining and promoting First Amendment rights of free
speech. Higher purpose goals are important because they connect
personal and team values with a purpose higher than dollars
and cents.

Work groups, and even many teams, that are goal-directed rely
almost exclusively on fixed target goals. By doing so, they miss the
additional benefits created by the different types of goals. To add
power to your team's goal setting and achievement, develop an
agenda that includes a mix of each of the five types of goals discussed.

6

CLARIFYING EXPECTATIONS FOR EXCEPTIONAL PERFORMANCE

In the early '80s I was seated next to a vice president of a very successful computer networking business who told me that when his company made a job offer to a prospective employee, the candidate was given a statement of the company's important values. If the candidate accepted the job, he or she would be agreeing to do business by those values. Employees were required to sign the statement, making it legally binding, with the understanding that any behavior which violated those values would become grounds for immediate dismissal.

Whenever I've shared that story with clients and others, I am always surprised that most people think the approach is harsh and the employer unreasonably demanding. But I believe it's the fairest approach possible. By establishing expectations in advance, the company gives potential employees a choice. No one is forced to work there; the company wants only those people who share its commitments and are confident they can live up to their employer's expectations and values.

When you clarify expectations in advance, you greatly increase the likelihood of having those expectations met. But many organizations paint a rosy picture for potential new hires. Employees take jobs only to discover later what is truly demanded and expected of them. They feel misled and cheated when faced with demands that they weren't aware of when they made the decision to join the company.

A team should be a place where members know what is expected of them *before they join*. They need to know upfront what their employer and fellow team members expect. Likewise, they need to understand what they can expect from their employer and teammates.

This doesn't mean developing detailed job descriptions for team members. Despite efforts to the contrary, most job descriptions are outdated, vague, and completely unused. If you already have job descriptions, don't throw them away. Somebody probably spent a lot of time and effort writing them. Instead, I'd suggest you make two additions to them—the only two job descriptions team members really need to succeed.

THE ONLY TWO JOB DESCRIPTIONS TEAM MEMBERS NEED

The manager of a large manufacturing plant learned about the limitations of typical job descriptions one day as he was roaming the shop floor. He noticed an obvious problem on the assembly line and turned to the nearest employee he could find. "Excuse me," he said, "there's a problem here that needs your attention." The employee responded, "Sorry, but it's not in my job description." The plant manager put his arm around the employee and said, "Son, listen carefully. I'm going to rewrite your job description for you today. Here it is: *Use your head.*"

Use your head. That may be the finest job description ever given. Certainly it is one of the most practical. The problem with many job descriptions is that they give people a place to hide and absolve them of taking personal responsibility for their actions and behaviors. Requiring team members to think makes them responsible for doing what needs to be done rather than what they're supposed to do.

The next time you're called upon to give a performance review, try this simplified approach. Meet with the team member two weeks in advance and explain that in the upcoming performance review, he or she will be given 30 minutes to answer one question. The team member can use any presentation technique he chooses: photographs, slides, an overhead projector, a written report—he can even bring people to testify on his behalf! Give the person two weeks to prepare for this question:

What have you done in the past review period to add value to this organization?

If your team members are like most people, the first time you ask this question they're going to look like a deer caught in the headlights of an oncoming automobile. Their eyes will get wide and they'll probably say something like "Whadaya mean? I've always done what you told me to do . . ." That's when you explain the shocking truth: computers and robots can be programmed to do what they're told. The unique and important contribution of every employee is to make him or herself valuable.

And that's the second job description: *Make yourself valuable.* The people who will survive in this very competitive world are those who add value to their organizations by making suggestions, implementing improvements, spotting and seizing opportunities, spearheading new projects, and building better relationships with fellow team members and customers.

(Why not design and teach a course for your team titled "How to Make Yourself Valuable"? Focus on what management feels are important "value-adding" skills and give team members plenty of specific ideas about what they can do to add value to the team and organization.)

ESTABLISHING EXPECTATIONS: THE 4 Cs

Expectations will vary, depending upon the team and its responsibilities. But one thing is certain: team members need to understand what it will take for them to successfully fulfill their roles, and the sooner expectations are clarified, the better.

Over the past several years, I have asked participants in my seminars to name the characteristics of an ideal team member. These participants have included team members and team leaders from practically every industry and work environment imaginable. Although their responses vary, I find that several characteristics consistently make the list. I have categorized these characteristics, which I call the 4 Cs of effective team members. They are: 1) Commitment; 2) Cooperation; 3) Communication; and 4) Contribution.

The First C Is Commitment. Commitment in a team environment means acting in a manner that supports the team's "holography": vision, mission, values, goals, and expectations. Commitment means giving this support even when doing so is difficult or unpleasant or comes at the expense of individual priorities. It is easy to be committed when there is no cost. True team commitment puts the best interests of the team first.

The Second C Is Cooperation. We can expect team members to cooperate when there is a sense of shared gain and common purpose.

81

We often equate cooperation with altruism. Altruistic behavior occurs when an individual helps without expecting anything in return. In almost any group, whether it's a team or not, you're going to have a few very helpful, altruistic people—but a few altruistic people do not a team make.

Teams are groups that have learned to cooperate to achieve a shared gain. In other words, I help you, knowing that you are equally willing to help me when appropriate or necessary. Since we have common goals, cooperating creates a common payoff. When a team senses no hope of shared gain, the best you can hope for is altruism. That's why it's important to link reward to performance. Team members need to know that, just as their employer counts on them, they too can count on their employer.

You may have played volleyball in the past, but have you ever played the game of cooperative volleyball? In cooperative volleyball, the objective is to keep the ball in the air. Success is judged on how many times you volley the ball back and forth across the net. In regular volleyball, when somebody scores a point, 50 percent of the people involved in the game are disappointed. In cooperative volleyball, everybody is happy when nobody loses! (I'll explain more about how to play cooperative volleyball in Chapter 8, along with two other games your group can play to develop teamwork.)

What's so neat about cooperative volleyball is that the enthusiasm of everyone is continuously high because people are working together toward a common purpose.

How can you tell if team members are cooperating? One way is to seek feedback. Here are four questions you can ask each team member to monitor levels of cooperation:

- Who actively assists and supports you?
- Who is somewhat supportive?

- Who doesn't assist or support?
- Is there anyone who actively works against you?

To prevent a tattletale session, always ask for specific examples of what the person referred to does or doesn't do. The objective is not to encourage people to get their coworkers in trouble, but to evaluate who are the team *players* and who are the team *slayers.* Some members may need individual coaching in cooperation skills or training on the dynamics of teamwork. Also, by asking these questions on a regular basis, you focus people on the cooperation expectation and remind them that the team places a high priority on cooperation.

The Third C Is Communication. In an industrial society, the strategic resource was capital. People with capital had the power. Now we live in an information age and the people with information have the power. That's one reason why a team member might be unwilling to share information with others—because it gives him or her power over them. But sharing information is critically important if the team is to succeed in an environment relatively free of power games.

In an autocratic environment, information is strategically given or withheld by those in control. This fosters mistrust and skepticism. In a team environment, the sharing of all relevant information builds trust and gives people what they need to know to make intelligent, informed decisions. In order to act quickly, the team must be able to communicate quickly. Complex systems of memos and formal responses don't make sense in a rapidly changing world. Team members need to be able to go directly to their teammates to give or get the information they need.

Another aspect of this communication expectation is a willingness to confront problems and conflict. Since problem solving and conflict resolution require interpersonal communication, team members must be expected—and taught—to handle the uncomfortable process of dealing with conflict.

The Fourth C Is Contribution. Contribution can never be an option.

The price of membership on any team is the
willingness to contribute to its success.

Allowing someone who is unwilling to contribute to stay on the team is one of the quickest ways to demoralize the rest of the team.

When employers hire new employees they're actually renting their behavior. Because you can't really buy commitment—it must be earned. But there are basic levels of performance that can indeed be bought. In an employment agreement, the employee promises certain behavior and the employer promises certain pay for that behavior—the metaphorical "rent." So what happens if an employer withholds rent—misses a pay period? The employee is justifiably outraged and demands payment. If that does not occur, the employee withholds further behavior and probably deals with this breach of contract in a court of law.

Yet every day in corporate America, employees withhold performance. It isn't that they can't perform, they just won't. They are doing less than they agreed to and less than they are paid for, but they get away with it because their employers let them. In other words, the employers keep paying the "rent."

THE MORTGAGE LENDER ANALOGY

Employers and team members should learn the mortgage lender approach. When I purchased my first house, I remember that at the closing, my mortgage lender said something to the effect of, "Mr. Sanborn, as long as you pay the mortgage, you get to stay in your new home. If you don't pay the mortgage, you don't get to stay." Of course she was much more diplomatic, but a clear understanding was established: when I signed the mortgage, giving what I promised was no longer an option.

Team members should be told at hiring—and sometimes need to be reminded from time to time—that if they don't contribute through their performance, they don't get to stay on the team. A team member who refuses to contribute is breaching his contractual agreement. To take it a step further, *any manager or team leader who allows a noncontributor to stay is guilty of not doing his or her job, either.* One of the tough things about team management is recognizing that we cannot sacrifice the good of the group for the good of an individual.

There are at least three devastating consequences of tolerating a team member who isn't contributing. First, it demoralizes the rest of the team. Nothing is more discouraging than showing up for work and getting paid no more than the person who goofs off. The second negative consequence is that you pass on to customers the additional overhead incurred by a noncontributor. Finally, if you are a government agency, you cheat the taxpayer, and if you are a publicly held company, you cheat the shareholder.

To Stay You Must Pay. The price includes commitment to the team and a willingness to cooperate, communicate, and contribute. The message for every team member and team leader is that contribution cannot be an option. It is a basic requirement for team membership.

THE SIX COMPONENTS OF STRONG TEAM RELATIONSHIPS

I've explained the four basic and necessary expectations of team members. There is, however, a higher goal that cannot be mandated so much as pursued and developed. It is building strong team relationships. You can reasonably expect a team member to communicate, but you can't necessarily expect her to feel camaraderie with the person she communicates with. There are some things team leadership and team members can do to enhance and improve their working relationships with each other. What follows is a model that, in reality, is seldom achieved. But knowing what ideally makes strong team relationships gives teambuilt organizations something to strive for.

Having studied what it takes to build successful relationships, particularly in a team environment, I've identified at least six necessary characteristics. The foundation for these characteristics goes back to the concept of commitment to the team, for without that, team members have little incentive to develop work relationships any stronger than those of traditional work groups. Scott Peck, therapist and best-selling author of *The Road Less Travelled,* says, "Commitment does not guarantee the success of a relationship. But it does more than any other factor to contribute to it."

Acceptance

The first characteristic is unconditional acceptance. Unconditional acceptance means accepting people as they are without asking or requiring them to change. Several years ago, I met a woman who was in charge of the education of incarcerated juveniles in Louisiana. Education is challenging in any environment, but her students had been convicted of felonies. In sharing her observations about human behavior, she said something I've never forgotten: "I'm not trying to make excuses for our kids. But I can tell you that, without exception, every kid in prison in this state feels that they were never accepted by their parents, by their friends, or by society. And that lack of acceptance has created a barrier that is nearly impossible for them to overcome."

An individual who does not feel accepted by the team faces a similar dilemma. By not initially accepting people as they are, we create a victimizing loop. The individual begins to feel that the only way he can be accepted is if he changes, but he has little reason to change until we accept him.

Don't confuse accepting the person with condoning his behavior. Acceptance recognizes that a person is worthwhile, even if we don't agree with everything he does.

Think about your own group or team. There are three forms of acceptance at work in most organizations. The most debilitating mode is *rejection* of people whose differences we do not like. This is an exclusionary practice that tragically and naïvely believes rejecting others increases the value of those we do accept. Since the rejected usually form their own groups, lack of acceptance simply creates cliques and factions in the organization that make it almost impossible to build teams.

The second form of acceptance is *tolerance.* As discussed earlier, even work groups are usually able to tolerate each other for practical reasons. While people do not necessarily feel excluded, neither do they feel included in the group, and therefore, they function independently. Unfortunately, synergy is seldom achieved by simply tolerating those you work with.

Teambuilt organizations achieve the third and highest form of acceptance, *valuing.* Individuals are accepted for who they are and valued for the contributions they are *capable* of making. This is an inclusionary practice that fosters the interdependence necessary for teamwork. Harold Burson, chairman of Burson Marsteller, the largest public relations firm in the world, says, "We prize the individual, but we celebrate the team." Teambuilt organizations consciously do both.

Time

The second characteristic necessary for strong team relationships is time. It's difficult to build relationships with people you seldom see or interact with personally. If you attempt to create teams composed of employees who work different shifts or in different facilities, you must invest the time to bring together periodically so they can get to know each other.

One formal but effective approach to this type of relationship building is the team retreat. Common practice is to hold one annually. I first experienced the value of team retreats when I was in the publishing business. The retreats started on Friday morning and ran through Sunday morning, which meant the company gave one day of its time and team members gave one day of theirs. Our team was permitted to invite spouses. We found that you got to know the people you worked with better if you knew the important people in their lives.

We always went away to a nice but not extravagant resort. This had two benefits. First, it minimized interruptions from ringing phones and visitors. Secondly, the resort setting created an atmosphere which suggested that we weren't just working, we were also being rewarded. The team retreat can, and should, be a perk for team members.

The focus of the retreat should be threefold: 1) evaluating past team performance, 2) planning for future team success, and 3) educating and motivating. (In the chapter on cooperation, I explain two games that can be used for experiential learning.) Make sure team members have a retreat agenda well in advance so they come prepared to participate. The biggest mistake you can make is not involving team members in the programming. When team leadership assumes all responsibility for presenting, it leaves little room for interaction, which is the most important component of the retreat.

Communication

The third characteristic of strong team relationships is communication. In Chapter 9, I explain the basics of effective team communication. But don't overlook the basics of effective interpersonal communications.

For interpersonal communication to be beneficial, the information must address one of three things: 1) behavior and performance, 2) relationships, and 3) outlook or attitude. Communication is beneficial when you can use it to improve the things you do, the people you have relationships with, or the attitude you possess.

Interpersonal communication should be emotionally honest—that means talking about not only what happened, but how we feel about what happened. Especially at work, we focus almost exclusively on what happened and ignore the emotional consequences. By ignoring how people feel, we eliminate an important dimension of relationship building.

Thirdly, our communication should be sensitive. It's possible to be sensitive and honest without being brutal. It has been said that tact is the ability to tell somebody to take a hike—and make them look forward to the trip. A communicator who is sensitive knows that:

> *You can't always tell people what they want to hear,*
> *but you can tell them in such a way that they'll be*
> *willing to listen.*

(More on this later.)

Effort

The fourth characteristic is effort. Relationships are hard work. But in this age of the microwave, we resist those things we can't attain instantly. Similarly, electronic data transmission takes place in a matter of seconds, so we're frustrated when it takes time and effort to create relationships with people.

If your organization has a sales force, note how much effort is expended developing relationships with customers. Why don't we make the same effort to develop strong relationships with team members?

How do you know if your team members are making an effort to build relationships? Look at how interpersonal problems are handled. The next time someone comes to you with a complaint about another team member that they'd like you to handle, ask what they've done to address the problem. If they haven't taken any action other than to complain to others, they aren't making the necessary effort.

If they have attempted to deal with the other person and their efforts have failed, ask a second question: "How did that person respond when you tried that?" Now you can determine if the problem is in the approach or if it lies with the other person.

To encourage team members to make an effort to get to know each other, run a monthly team members' spotlight. This isn't an "employee of the month" type of recognition—the spotlight simply focuses on getting to know a different team member. Each month, have a different team member interview the person who's "in the spotlight." Prepare a simple form with the kind of information they should be getting: past work experience, families, community involvement, hobbies. Then write up a brief article that can appear in the team newsletter or be posted on the team bulletin board. Headline it, "This month, get to know . . ." Make sure you let the team member review the article before it appears, so he or she is comfortable with what's being written. Consider including a photo of the person involved in a favorite activity outside work.

If you think it's silly to post a team member spotlight, you need to hang around the lunchroom bulletin board. I've seen employees so bored they'll take time to read OSHA regulations, just because they're posted. Why not take advantage of an opportunity to make positive information available—and don't worry about the cynics.

Sometimes what team leadership considers a lack of effort is actually a lack of skill. Maybe you've got one team member who has been trained in conflict resolution. Another has attended a seminar on interpersonal communication, and a third has become very skilled at customer service. Give team members an opportunity to learn from each other, to share skills and knowledge. The only thing better than one team member skilled at conflict resolution, for example, is an entire team of people who understand the basics of constructively dealing with conflict.

To build strong relationships, address the knowledge differences between team members. Then schedule team learning. If we want people to grow together, they need to learn together. Occasionally bring in a seminar for the entire team or send them all out for a seminar.

If you can't send the whole team for training, make sure the representative you send has a chance to share what he's learned when he comes back. My first boss used to call it a debriefing. The team member would be given 10 to 15 minutes at the team meeting to highlight the most important things learned. This reinforced his learning and gave team members who couldn't attend a useful overview. Direct learning is still the best option, but there is value in vicarious learning as well.

Conflict Resolution

The fifth characteristic of strong relationships is conflict resolution. Healthy teams do not sweep conflict under the carpet. They deal with it quickly and efficiently.

However, just as people can take conflict too lightly, it can become too serious. Sometimes team members get caught up in conflicts that really aren't that important. Some conflicts are simply *annoying*. Say you've got a team member who cracks his knuckles. It drives you nuts. But as my grandfather always said, "It's an inconvenience, but it's not fatal." In other words, you might ask him to stop, but if he doesn't, don't sweat it.

Other conflicts are *noteworthy*. Noteworthy conflicts have significant consequences for the team; if those consequences are noticeable enough, at some point you should work through the conflict. But there is no urgency, since the conflict isn't taking away from the team's ability to get the job done.

Save your energy for the most significant type of conflict— *debilitating* conflicts that significantly hamper the team's ability to produce results. If you don't worry about the annoying conflicts and spend little time on the noteworthy conflicts, you'll have time and energy to spend on the high-priority, debilitating conflicts.

Forgiveness

The sixth characteristic necessary for strong team relationships is forgiveness. "Everybody makes mistakes" and "Nobody's perfect" are more often used in self-defense than when another team member trespasses against us. Some team members believe in "burying the hatchet," but, to quote a country western song by Garth Brooks, they ". . . leave the handle sticking out."

True forgiveness means taking an uncommon approach to mistakes and grievances:

> *Don't forgive people for the little injustices and the*
> *petty mistakes that they commit. Just don't remember*
> *those injustices and mistakes to begin with.*

Until team members can learn to "forgive or forget," it will be difficult to overcome the indifference that continually arises when trying to make teamwork work.

TEAM ROLES

In a teambuilt organization, team members know what is expected and have a clear sense of what it takes to develop strong team relationships. But there are many roles team members can play in creating synergistic teamwork. In some instances, team members naturally fulfill these roles. In other situations, a team member has the potential to fulfill these roles if encouraged. Here are some of the roles team leaders should identify, develop, and encourage in team members.

I am not suggesting labeling, which limits an individual's growth by confining the person to a behavior or characteristic, usually negative, that may or may not be true. In this situation, the emphasis should be on the positive things team members already bring, or have the potential to bring, to enhance overall team performance. Consider these roles less responsibilities than opportunities.

Club Med, the company that runs highly successful international resorts, has a staff member at each location whose title is *animator.* It is the animator's responsibility to keep things lively. Part entertainer, part schmoozer, animators mix with the guests to inject fun and humor into whatever is going on. Teams are fortunate when they have one or more people who are informal animators.

The *encourager* is great at recognizing when team members need to hear a good word. They spot the good work of others and take time to comment. A team leader can overcome terminal discouragement if an encourager offers positive feedback that others have failed to provide.

A *stabilizer* is easy to spot but hard to define. In the midst of chaos, the stabilizer is the person who keeps the team from buffeting out of control. Often they are transcendent personalities who are quietly competent. Not only are stabilizers difficult to fluster, they can calm the most unglued teammate when necessary.

"Groupthink" won't be a problem if someone on your team is a *challenger.* This person is sometimes annoying because she enjoys playing the role of devil's advocate. The challenger's motivation, however, is to make sure ideas are tested and true. Here comments open up new perspectives and frequently improve on the idea she was initially challenging.

While the challenger's realm is the intellect, the *innovator* is action-oriented. These people spot opportunities for improvement and, if nobody else is seizing them, do it themselves. But, like the challenger, they abhor the status quo.

Some team members have highly developed problem-solving skills. They fulfill the role of *troubleshooter.* Most people can spot problems. But the troubleshooter is expert at identifying the real cause and coming up with workable solutions. When something goes wrong, team members look for the troubleshooter.

The *sage* is an excellent listener. You might think they give lots of advice, but the sage's biggest strength is the ability to listen to others and really hear what they're saying. When sages finally do give advice, more often than not, it comes in the form of questions that encourage people to look at a situation from a different perspective.

There are other roles that team members can and do play. The savvy team leader is one who encourages and reinforces those positive attributes that are inherent in others.

7

THE ATTRIBUTES OF LEGENDARY TEAM LEADERSHIP

What do we expect of team leaders? More importantly, what *should* we expect?

"Management"—used interchangeably and mistakenly with the term "leadership"—often seems officebound. Certainly they wouldn't make the decisions they do if they ever spent time in the real world where the work gets done. Employees often marvel at the large salaries managers command, despite much evidence that they do little more than shuffle paperwork and sign off on decisions. But if something goes wrong, they're close by to chew out the offending party.

In the 1960s, Norman Maier of the University of Michigan did research on the factors that contribute to group performance. He found that the primary determinant of a team's success was the skill of the person leading it. One can further conclude (you probably already did) that the success of an organization is, to a large extent, determined by the skill of the managers leading it. (Although all too frequently, employees succeed in spite of management, not because of them. The human spirit can triumph over bad leadership, but it shouldn't have to.) Robert Townsend, author and former CEO of Avis Rent-a-Car, once said, "Most people today are administered, not led. They're treated like personnel, rather than people."

DEFINING LEADERSHIP

Let's define leadership. Before you read further, write in two sentences or less your definition of leadership in the space below:

Leadership: _____

_____

Trumpeter Louis Armstrong was once asked to define jazz, and he replied, "Brother, if you can't feel it, I can't define it." Leadership is a lot like jazz—we recognize it when we see it, and from time to time we experience it, but when somebody asks us to define it, we struggle with the words.

One of my favorite definitions comes from Bill Holekamp, general manager of an Enterprise Rent-A-Car operation in Southern California. Holekamp says, "Leadership is understanding who your people really work for—themselves—and giving them stuff."

I asked him to elaborate on what he meant by "stuff." He gave these examples: encouragement, support, resources, coaching, appreciation, and recognition. Holekamp believes that if you give people what they need to be successful, they'll succeed.

In our society, we associate leadership with *getting*—getting results, respect, trust, and loyalty. Holekamp's definition is about *giving*. We get results from team members because we give them what they need to produce results. Teams respect leaders who respect them. Gen. H. Norman Schwarzkopf said of his success during

Operation Desert Storm, "I built trust among (military officers) because I trusted them."

> *The reality of leadership is that giving almost always*
> *precedes getting.*

Here's my working definition of leadership: *Leadership is the ability to help individuals or organizations surpass themselves.*

Leadership enables individuals or organizations do more, and be more, than they would without your influence. The root word of "management" means "to handle." Management is about handling people and resources, and if we lived in a world that never changed, managerial skills alone would suffice. By comparison, the root word of leadership means "to go." Leadership is about taking people and organizations from where they are to where they could be. In a rapidly changing world, it is the leader's responsibility to help team members get from where they are to their destination—the team's vision.

(Here's some homework: Ask each of your team members to define leadership. Find out what they expect a leader to be and do. The results will be a gritty but pragmatic definition you can use in your leadership development.)

Growing People

Would you like to add members to your team without increasing your payroll? Let's assume there are 10 on your team. If your leadership helps each of those 10 team members become 10 percent better over the next 12 months, you will have created an entire unit of human contribution. With only 10 on the payroll, you've now got the output of 11. Leadership is about doing more with what you already have.

The Leader's Perspective

The relationship between Helen Keller and her teacher, Anne Sullivan, is legendary. Sullivan helped Keller become one of the greatest figures of her time when others before her had attempted to work with the blind and deaf girl and failed. What accounted for Sullivan's success? Until Sullivan, the question had always been, "What will we do *with* Helen?" Sullivan asked: "What can I do *for* Helen?" The difference in perspective changed Keller's life.

Similarly, too much of management's thinking is preoccupied with the question, "What will we do with our work force?" The objective is to increase productivity, decrease costs, and prevent problems. Little time is devoted to the question, "What will we do for our workforce?" Holekamp's suggestion that leadership is about giving employees "stuff" is what differentiates leaders from managers.

The hard-core manager responds with rhetoric along the lines of "This isn't a charity, it's a business," and "I don't believe in coddling my people." Doing for employees isn't about charity and coddling. It is about understanding the reality of the marketplace. Few employees work for free. Most organizations pay their employees, and to be competitive, they must pay competitively. What differentiates organizations is how leadership treats employees, not how much they pay them. Leadership is about giving team members a chance to make a living and a life.

AN AGENDA FOR TEAM LEADERSHIP

A leader whose perspective is doing for employees must learn certain basic skills to be effective. Here's an agenda to help you develop the foundational skills of team leadership. Once you've mastered these you can work on enhancing and fine-tuning your leadership techniques.

Agenda Item #1: Take Care of Team Members

While staying at a very well known hotel in the Chicago area, I noticed that almost every interaction I had with employees was negative. I was treated either poorly or with incredible incompetence. One nice exception was the woman who served my lunch. When I told her about my other experiences at the hotel, she explained that management and employees had a very antagonistic relationship. "I could have guessed as much," I said. "You can usually predict the level of service you will receive as a customer based on the way management treats the employees who deliver that service." She agreed and went on to reveal that employee morale was very low because of management's highly authoritarian and inconsiderate treatment.

The leader sets the tone for how team members treat each other and the people they serve. Leaders need interpersonal skills to meet the self-esteem needs of team members. It is unrealistic to expect team members to serve their customers, whether internal or external, better than they are treated themselves.

One company that understands this is Hyatt Hotels. Hyatt has been surveying its employees for the past 15 years. With more than 100 items, the questionnaire asks seven key questions, such as "Tell us what you think of management." Employees' answers make up the general morale index, or GMI. Hyatt's survey results show that hotels with the highest GMI scores also get the highest ratings from customers and the highest sales and gross operating profits.

What do team members need to succeed? Let's look at three basic but critically important needs shared by most team members: recognition, belonging, and support.

Take the Need for Recognition. William James, the American psychologist, believed that roughly 85 percent of an adult's behavior is designed to get others to notice. In fact, the need for attention is so strong that if someone cannot attract positive attention, he or she will resort to negative behavior—because negative attention is better than no attention at all.

At the height of the punk rock movement, a journalist interviewed a young woman who was obviously very attractive, despite the garish makeup and multi-colored spiky hair. The journalist commented that the young lady was naturally attractive and then asked why she chose the unusual appearance. "I'd rather be looked at than looked over," she said.

But team leaders often fail to understand this basic human need. Some of the team leaders I work with find it difficult to reward and recognize support staff who have limited job responsibilities and often repetitive work. The leaders feel that job enrichment is difficult, and the nature of the work makes it tough to link pay to performance. But appreciation is certainly a form of recognition.

Take Gladys. Well into her 50s, Gladys has held the same secretarial position for many years. Yet her enthusiasm for her work and employer remains strong. "Let me tell you about my boss," she says. "For the last several years, our team of four has reported to him. At the end of every day—no matter how hectic or trying things have been—he comes by each of our desks and says, 'Thank you for another good day.' " Clearly it matters to Gladys that her boss genuinely appreciates his team's contributions.

The Second Important Need Team Members Have Is Belonging.
There's a wonderful "Far Side" cartoon by Gary Larson that shows thousands of identical penguins standing on an ice floe. Right in the middle of the group is one penguin standing up a little bit taller, singing, "I gotta be me, I just gotta be me. . . ."

This cartoon wonderfully illustrates our need for standing out while still belonging. We all want to be part of a community. There is safety and security in interdependence. Paradoxically, we also want to stand out, to be seen as individuals, and valued for who we are and what we do.

One of the needs psychologist Abraham Maslow identified in his now famous and often quoted "hierarchy of needs" was the social need—association with and acceptance by other people. Maslow believed we have an innate need for community and belonging, to be a part of something bigger than ourselves. Being a part of a winning team is one way to meet that need.

Organizations tend to meet either individual or belonging needs but seldom do a good job of meeting both. Reward systems that recognize individuals are easier to administer than those that recognize cooperative effort. In rewarding teamwork, we often ignore the contributions of team members. Leaders must consistently and creatively meet both the need for belonging and the need for individual recognition.

The Third Critical Need Is Support. If you really want to get commitment from your people, go to the wall for them. If you really want to get commitment, be willing to take some heat for them. American business management teaches two important lessons. One we've learned very well, the other not at all. The first lesson is that team leaders, or managers, are supposed to represent the organization's needs to their team members. That's the lesson we've learned well. The one we've learned poorly is that the manager or team leader is supposed to represent the team's needs to the organization. Sometimes that means we have to creatively bend or break the rules.

If the system doesn't work, then work the system.

Team leaders frequently complain that they aren't authorized to give their team members the support they need. But a true leader knows when and how to champion his team.

Take this scenario: Monday morning your boss calls you into his office and proceeds to tell you that he's just learned of a rush project that absolutely must be done by 6 P.M. Wednesday. He gives you this motivational send-off: "Just get it done!"

You head back to your department to rally the team. You explain the situation. According to your calculations, if everybody works 18 hours a day for the next three days, you might be able to pull it off. You ask for volunteers. Unfortunately, you're still in the early stages of teambuilding and only one person, Jane, is willing to work late. You and Jane work until 11 P.M. Monday, 10:30 P.M. Tuesday, and Jane is standing with you Wednesday as you wave goodbye to the Fed Ex driver who will deliver the completed project to your big client.

Jane has done an exceptional job and she deserves exceptional treatment. Because she's a salaried employee, you can't pay her overtime—and even if you could, it would be an insufficient gesture. After thinking about it some, you realize that Jane not only deserves Friday off, she probably needs the day to recuperate. The problem: organizational policy prevents you from giving employees time off.

Now's the time to work the system, if you're a champion of your team members. You call Jane into your office Thursday morning and tell her how much you appreciated her help on the special project, that you couldn't have done it without her. To express that appreciation, you're asking her to take Friday to do some special "field work." Jane is puzzled and wants to know what "field work" is. You tell her field work is anything she wants it to be. She perks up and asks if you are giving her the day off. You explain that you need to be very clear: you can't give her the day off because it is against the policy, but nothing prohibits you from asking her to do field work. A knowing smile crosses Jane's face—she understands that you're taking care of her.

Friday morning Jane doesn't show up for work and you get a visit from the company "rules troll." The troll exists for one reason only—to make sure that nobody breaks the rules. "Where's Jane?" the troll demands. You calmly reply that she's out doing field work.

Luckily, rules trolls aren't very bright, but they are suspicious. The troll investigates and eventually learns that what you called "field work" was really a day off and that you broke a serious rule. Now what happens?

Probably not much. Maybe your boss chews you out and tells you not to do it again. It's unlikely that this would be grounds for dismissal. If you're feeling particularly assertive, you might point out that Jane helped complete the special project at significant personal sacrifice and that, furthermore, if you hadn't given her Friday off, you could pretty much forget that kind of commitment from her next time the company found itself in a clutch situation.

The moral of this story:

> *Insubordination is breaking a rule for personal gain.*
> *Championing is breaking a rule to give team members*
> *the support they deserve.*

Sometimes supporting your team members means flexing or even breaking the rules. It means you might have to take some heat so your team members don't. But if you aren't willing to go to the wall for them, don't expect them to do that for you. Team members need your support. Management expects you to represent the needs of the organization to your team. Your team needs you to represent their needs to management.

Agenda Item #2: Take Care of Business

What the company needs from your team is results. Managers seem to think there is a conflict between focusing on people and focusing on results. Leaders know this is never a clear-cut choice. You've got to keep one eye on results and the other eye on your people.

If you are a team leader who is well-liked and popular with team members but you aren't accomplishing results, you're probably regarded as a good old boy or gal who's ineffectual. In this age of cutbacks and layoffs, good old boys and gals usually have a very short shelf life. If, however, you are the kind of leader who always meets the organization's goals at your team's expense—high levels of stress and burnout and low levels of fun—you're probably known as a tyrant or worse.

Learning to balance the needs of your team members with the needs of the organization may be the toughest part of team leadership. But it's an essential leadership skill.

Agenda Item #3: Communication Is Critical

Ask someone to name the skills of leadership, and communication invariably makes the list. The problem is that we commonly interpret communication as the ability to express oneself clearly. The bigger challenge is to understand team members accurately. Team leaders must be able to do both, express and understand.

There are many reasons why listening is so tough in corporate America today. Only one out of every 10 people has ever had any formal listening training, even though experts say *one listening course can improve the ability to comprehend by 25 to 40 percent.* We spend 45 percent of our waking hours listening—to coworkers, bosses, team members, and others. But without that, the most frequently used communication tool is the least taught.

What's more, when something is said to us, we immediately forget 45 to 50 percent of it. That means we may be making important decisions on the basis of information that is nearly 50 percent incomplete—which explains why bad decisions occur.

Perhaps the main reason management doesn't listen well is much more gritty than a simple lack of skill: management is afraid of what they'll hear. Reality can be distasteful and ignorance really can be bliss—for a while. If you don't ask team members for input, you won't run the risk of disagreements. If you don't ask them for ideas, you won't have to deal with dumb ideas (of course, you won't get any smart ones either). If you don't ask your team for feedback on your leadership style, you won't be criticized (at least not to your face).

Management doesn't listen well because they don't want to hear. Maybe that's why quality expert Tom Peters defines listening as "empowering employees by taking them seriously."

> *Team leaders need to be interested enough to ask,*
> *respectful enough to listen, and caring enough to*
> *respond.*

While researching a client firm on the East Coast, I found that all the managers at one of their plants shared an intense dislike for their operations manager. Two were candid enough to share the reason: "She sits in her office all day. If you have a problem or an idea, you have to go to her. She never comes to you. She doesn't ask what you think, and seems to lord it over you when you go in to see her. Trying to communicate with her has become such a ceremony we call it 'going before the throne of God.'" Ironically, the manager they referred to was very competent—and even responded to their questions and ideas. But what really irritated them was that she never seemed interested in their ideas and opinions.

To be an effective communicator, a team leader needs to care enough about members to ask them what's important. Whether you use formal means, such as suggestion systems or scheduled one-on-one meetings, or informal means, such as hanging out with team members and schmoozing, you need to be interested enough to ask.

When you do ask for ideas and suggestions, you'll get a few intentional duds. Responses to "What would make this a better place to work?" might include "Beer available at all times," or "Shoot management." A manager would use such responses as proof that "it just doesn't pay to ask because they don't take us seriously." A true leader knows a few weird ideas are inevitable, gets a chuckle out of them, and then concentrates on the solid ideas.

A word of warning: If you're not sure you can handle feedback, it's better not to solicit it. To ask, then not accept honest feedback is devasting to the giver. Even if you don't agree with what you hear, it is vitally important that you reward the team members' honesty by accepting what they say at face value. We all hesitate to be honest when we know we are going to suffer for it later. If you ask for input and do anything less than accept and respect what you get, don't bother asking again. Your team will have learned that you're not to be believed when you say you want to know what they think.

The biggest reward you can give team members for sharing their ideas is to respond appropriately. At the very least, that means acknowledging their ideas and thanking them. But the best payoff is implementing part or all of their ideas.

Agenda Item #4: Emphasize Values and Expectations

In the section on developing a holographic team, I said that values define the team's integrity and provide a basis for decision making and actions. But how does a leader actively promote those values? One way is to become a storyteller. Every day, look for two or three examples of somebody on your team or in your organization who is living the values. Note incidents and events that typify those values in action. And then tell everybody. Don't leave it to chance that others will find out—spread the good news yourself.

While you're looking for these values stories, you'll also notice chinks in the team's armor. Don't hesitate to point out inconsistencies and opportunities for improvement. Tell a dramatic story about how the team failed a customer and what it meant to the customer. Call somebody on the carpet if the team believes in participative decision making and that person is pushing a decision through autocratically. As a team leader, one of your jobs is to spotlight values in action; another is to look for the inconsistencies that would sink you.

No doubt you've run across the admonition "inspect what you expect." I'm concerned about what managers expect from their teams, because often it isn't much.

Robert Rosenthal and Lenore Jacobson reported in *Pygmalion in the Classroom* that teachers' high expectations of their students were enough to cause an increase in overall IQ. Team leaders need to remember the power of expectations and use the Pygmalion effect in the workplace:

> *Expect more from your team and you'll get more. You may not get all of what you expected, but you'll get more than you would have.*

Agenda Item #5: Make It a Point to Grow Replacements

Are you such an excellent manager that your employer sees you as irreplaceable? If the answer is yes, you're probably in big trouble. Someday upper management is going to think about promoting you, and they'll have to consider who to move into your current role as manager/team leader. Then the reality will hit them: nobody on your team could do the job. You've got a terrific team of followers but not one of them has learned how to lead. With no replacement available, they're going to have to keep you there forever!

Should that unfortunate scenario ever occur, you will have learned an important lesson the hard way:

> *Team leaders can become victims of their own competency.*

Team leaders become too good when there is no one else capable of replacing them. In their pursuit of leadership excellence, they have missed an important point: leaders need to groom a replacement. Shortsighted leaders focus only on developing "followership" in team members.

One of the best ways to groom a replacement is a technique I call *shared leadership.* Shared leadership means that you provide team members with opportunities to lead on a regular basis. For example, sometimes let a member conduct a team meeting. Or put another team member in charge of a special project. Look for opportunities to delegate decision making, such as asking someone to deal with an unhappy customer. Give the person the authority to use his judgment to do whatever he thinks is necessary to make the customer happy. You can even appoint a team member to represent your team at an interdepartmental meeting.

Just make sure you share tasks typically reserved for a team leader. One of the best ways to learn how to lead is by leading. If you routinely practice shared leadership, over time you'll develop some leaders among the followers. (You may need to explain why you are sharing leadership responsibilities, so team members don't think you're trying to lighten your load at their expense.) Just don't wait until it is too late: groom a replacement—or better yet, replacements—starting now.

Agenda Item #6: Develop People and Pursue Progress

Goethe said, "Treat people as though they were what they ought to be and you help them become what they are capable of being."

Team leaders should be able to see future potential in team members, not just present performance.

It's easy to assess how well a team member is doing; the challenge is to look beyond the present and determine when a team member is capable of more. A team leader who can help an employee deal with inner limitations and change the way he sees himself has the power to influence significant, if not radical, improvement. A recurrent phrase team members use in interviews about effective leadership is "He or she believes in me." Sometimes they even say the leader believed in them more than they believed in themselves.

As a speaker and seminar leader, I've noticed that people tend to resist anything that isn't psychologically complicated. So what I'm about to share may not be complicated enough to convince you it's true. But if you want to increase the performance of your team immediately, dedicate two days a year for intensive one-on-one coaching with each member. By devoting two full days per team member, you will probably increase your one-on-one coaching time by at least 12 to 18 hours. Typically the only one-on-one coaching most employees receive occurs during a performance appraisal or a review. Even then, little is done to actually increase or develop the skills and abilities of employees.

> *To pursue progress, keeping asking, "Is the team*
> *making progress or regress?"*

You must challenge yourself and your team to continually examine the way you perform. Take your operation apart piece by piece, nut by nut, bolt by bolt, and ask yourselves, *"How can we do it all even better?"*

Agenda Item #7: Model Behavior

The shortest leadership definition on record comes from Albert Schweitzer, who said, "Example is leadership."

Several years ago I met an unusual entrepreneur from Detroit. He and two friends had left their corporate management positions to start a small service firm which grew to almost 50 employees. From the beginning, they had implemented an innovative policy: an employee couldn't work after regular business hours without first notifying the three partners. The entrepreneur explained: "My partners and I were tired of working long hours for managers who went home before we did or who were out on the golf course. We decided the best way to get commitment was to make sure we worked as long and hard as our most dedicated employees. As a result, we don't let anybody work late alone. At least one of us stays late too. Often we'll order a pizza or Chinese food and have dinner with our people who have put in extra time. We want to make sure that everybody knows nobody works harder than we do."

These entrepreneurs have cracked the code of leadership. The most powerful technique available to any team leader is a willingness to model the behavior and commitment desired from team members. You cannot reasonably expect people to be more committed, work harder, or be more enthusiastic than you are willing to be.

Agenda Item #7: Deal with Difficulty

Effective team leadership requires the ability to deal with problem members. One of the most pressing problems: what to do with people who don't want to be a part of the team.

I'm frequently asked how to handle people who weren't given a choice about being on a team. For instance, a sudden change in management direction requires them to become contributing members of a team. But these employees feel that as long as they do their work, nobody should bother them. My response has always been that requiring teamwork from people who have never been exposed to the concept is self-defeating. That's why I outlined the steps to getting started in teamwork in Chapter 2. But what if you've done all those things and someone still chooses not to participate?

Try creating a non-team. Depending on the type of work a person does, it may be possible to allow him or her to work with limited interaction with others. Non-team members are given very clear instructions about what needs to be done, but they are not evaluated on their willingness to cooperate. Likewise, they don't benefit from the interdependence that regular team members do. Most people, I believe, will tire of this scenario quickly and ask for an opportunity to be part of their original team.

If you are unwilling or unable to create a non-team, you might want to ask the resistant employee this question: "If you can't fundamentally buy into teamwork, are you thinking about another place of employment?" It sounds like a threat, but it isn't really. It is an honest appraisal of the situation.

*If your organization is going to become teambuilt,
people who don't share that interest and commitment
are going to be mighty unhappy.*

Explain that if someone isn't comfortable with the teamwork concept, it would be a good time to seek employment somewhere else. Then be willing to help your employee do so.

It can get worse. The employee might stay, and you might have to keep him. There's no non-team to put him on. His resistance isn't enough to merit asking him to leave, and he doesn't want to leave anyhow. He decides to stick it out but his participation is marginal, if not counterproductive. The danger is that he will become a *team slayer*.

DEALING WITH TEAM SLAYERS

Whenever a problem arises with a team member, there are certain steps a leader should take before acting. While the specifics of every situation will vary, here's a basic approach you can use to determine what's wrong and what should be done.

Before you can alleviate any symptom, you need to diagnose its cause. Why isn't this person cooperating? What's causing the lack of participation?

To accurately diagnose the problem, you need to involve the team member. That's your second step—to *discuss* the situation. Explain your motivation. Hopefully he'll respect that you value him enough to confront the problem. Ask specific questions that get beneath the surface, and be prepared to take any ownership you may have in the problem. For example, you may be causing the problem by the way you treat him or because of some failure to notice his needs. Look for what you can do to create a positive change.

Then *coach* the team member on the things that need to be done to successfully resolve the situation. Explain what you'll do and determine specific actions he'll need to take to make the relationship work.

The next step is critically important. Coaching won't do any good unless you *get an agreement* from the team member about the behavior that will change. What action will he commit to taking as a result of your discussion? If you don't get an agreement, you're going to find yourself going through the diagnosis, discussion, and coaching procedures over and over and over without any significant behavioral change.

As part of the agreement, determine a realistic time frame for the behavior change to take place. Then positively or negatively *reinforce* when he is or isn't doing what he's agreed to.

Finally, if despite your best coaching, agreement, and reinforcement, the team slayer still won't do what's necessary to maintain the relationship, the only option left is removal. The good of the team can't be sacrificed for the benefit of an individual who is unwilling to do his part. The group's needs should supersede the individual's needs, especially when you've done everything humanly possible to be fair in dealing with the problem.

Anticipating a Removal

If you've determined that somebody needs to be removed from the team, should you inform him that this is a possibility when you're discussing the problem? To be an effective team leader, one of the things you should talk about is what will happen if his behavior doesn't change.

Whenever I suggest to someone that removal is an option, my intent is not intimidation—I just want to be honest. I'm letting the person know that I want to give him a reasonable period of time, but there's definitely a limit to how long he'll have to change. I suggest that before you ever terminate someone, give the person a probationary period. This offers him a chance to realize that one negative consequence of his unwillingness to change is potential removal from the team.

8

STEP 3: COOPERATE

Baseball legend Casey Stengel once said, "It's easy to get good players. Getting them to play together, that's the hard part." Stengel might have been overly optimistic about finding good players, but he was right about how difficult it is to get them to play together.

Coordinating the efforts of a team to harness synergy is one of hardest jobs in making teamwork work. Even understanding what is important to the team and sharing a commitment to the team's success isn't enough to assure that team members will do what needs to be done. The team needs an action plan.

ACTION PLANNING

The holographic team understands the team vision, purpose, values, goals, and expectations. Field Marshal Erwin Rommel once said that the best strategic plan is totally useless unless it can be executed tactically. Consider the action plan for your strategy. Strategy is the art of designing a plan to achieve a goal; action items are anything a team members does to implement the strategy.

Action planning enables a team to accomplish more of what they talk about doing.

Any time the team meets, someone should be taking notes that can be used to complete the action plan. Here's a sample plan: Set up a chart with five columns. Label the column heads as: Project; Action Item; Team Member(s); Due Date; Comments.

The first column identifies the major project or goal discussed at the meeting. The second column breaks the project into action items: specific steps that must be taken to achieve the desired results. The third column assigns responsibility.

A number of ideas are discussed at any team meeting. As participants, team members may get a pretty good idea of what needs to be done but not know for sure who is supposed to do it. One of the best ways to increase team productivity is to make specific people responsible for completely accomplishing an action item. People need to be clear on what is expected of them. When everyone has accomplished their action items, the project comes together like pieces of a puzzle.

The fourth column creates a sense of urgency by noting the date that each action item is to be completed. The fifth column can be used for any miscellaneous notes about decision-making authority, resources needed, or the like.

As team leader, you could add additional columns to your action plan. One column could be an inspection date to make sure that action items will be completed on time. Another column might note when the action item was actually accomplished—some team members might finish early, others on time, a few late. This information will be useful later in coaching sessions with individual team members. By reviewing action plans, you will be able to spot team members who are being overworked or underutilized, and maintain a more balanced and fair workload.

At the end of each meeting, the action plan should be typed and distributed to team members before the end of the working day. Now you have a record of what was discussed and what must be done.

Monitoring the action plan will ensure that something happens after the meeting.

THE MISSING LINK: QTWs

Action planning provides a workable strategy for achieving your team goals. Large accomplishments are the result of cumulative little successes. The building blocks of an action plan are QTWs: *quick team wins.*

After a goal setting/action planning session, team members are enthused. But sometimes they lose their enthusiasm within a few days if they haven't been able to make discernible progress toward their goals. Getting started is the most difficult part, and QTWs are the missing link that prevents most goals from being achieved.

Quick team wins are actions that team members can take immediately to start moving closer to the long-range goals. By determining specific steps that can be taken within 24 hours, team members have concrete actions they can take to begin. And by taking immediate action, you can create immediate momentum toward ultimate success.

If you can prove to people they can win in little ways,
it will be easier for them to win in bigger and bigger
ways.

Often the missing ingredient in long-term goal setting is short-term action planning. QTWs show people what they can start doing immediately to convert plans to progress.

DECISION MAKING THE TEAMBUILT WAY

Decision making is very important in creating teamwork, because how decisions are made will affect three things: the *quality* of the decision, the *speed* with which the decision is made and implemented, and the team's *commitment* to the decision.

The Quest for Quality. In an autocratic environment, the person with the most expertise makes the decisions. A study done by the Hay Group, the University of Michigan, and a strategic planning institute found that organizations which drew a broad range of executives into the decision-making process were more profitable and enjoyed greater return on their investments than organizations with a single autocratic decision maker.

The Need for Speed. Autocratic decision makers make decisions more quickly than groups do. But the time lost by involving the group in making the decision is time gained in implementing the decision. That's the group trade-off—longer decision making but faster implementation.

The Cost of Commitment. Commitment is always higher when the decision involves everyone who will be affected by it. Within a team, there are basically three types of decisions: unilateral, consultative, and group.

A unilateral decision is made by an individual. You might think that a book about teamwork would not include a discussion of this type of decision, but there are times when it's appropriate. Make a *unilateral decision* when:

- A team member is solely responsible for the outcome of the decision and does not need other team members' support to achieve it.
- Time is limited. In a hectic environment, it may not be possible to include others and still make the decision quickly.
- The decision could not be improved by involving others. Sometimes a team member will possess a specific level of expertise that makes them uniquely qualified to make a certain decision.

The second way to make decisions is what I call *consultative decision*. A consultative decision is made by an individual with input from others. Use a consultative decision when:

- You lack expertise or think more expertise would be helpful.
- You don't have enough time to involve everybody in the process.
- You want to communicate to people that their opinions count. While they won't actually be involved in making the decision, you certainly want to represent their points of view when the decision is made.

The third option is the *group decision,* or consensus. It makes sense to use a group decision-making process when:

- The people who are going to be affected by the decision need to be committed to it.
- You have sufficient time, or can at least set aside time, to include the group.
- The expertise of the group will contribute to the outcome of the decision.

The key is to use a mix. If you make only unilateral decisions, you'll create an autocratic, nonparticipative environment. If you make only group decisions, you'll have management by committee—and we all know that has a bad reputation. People will not mind the unilateral and consultative decisions if they know that when an important decision affecting the team is made, they will be involved.

When you are called upon to make day-to-day decisions, use a mix of unilateral, consultative, and group decisions. That is the key to gaining cooperation among your team members.

CONFLICT

Conflict is never a question of "if" but a question of "when." What matters most in teamwork is how the team responds. Do they cope with conflict independently, competitively, or cooperatively?

There are several approaches for dealing with conflict, but each considers these two basic needs: the outcome or resolution of the conflict, and the relationship with other team members.

Avoidance doesn't allow for any resolution (although you could say that no resolution is a resolution). Avoidance can be hard on team relationships by frustrating others who may want something to be done. One instance where avoidance makes sense: when the conflict is trivial or insignificant. Avoidance can be particularly useful when time is limited, and members would find themselves bogged down if they tried to resolve every conflict.

Giving in to another team member usually means accepting their solution to the conflict. You won't get the outcome you desired, but you will maintain the relationship by letting the other person have what was important to him. Giving in all the time can be a sign of unhealthy passivity, but it is a rational strategy when the relationship you have with another team member is more important than getting your way.

Competing seeks to win a solution you desire. It can be, and usually is, hard on the relationship you have with the other person. When matters of principle are involved—you are committed to your position on ethical grounds, for example—it may be necessary to compete. Sometimes competition achieves what is best for the team, especially if some team members have taken self-serving positions in the conflict.

Compromise is a popular conflict-resolution strategy. It means giving up some of what you want to get some of what you want. Although a useful approach when time is limited, it often falls short of the better outcome that could be achieved with a little more effort.

Cooperation is an approach that seeks to integrate the needs of all parties in the conflict and come up with solutions that creatively meet those needs. Not only are relationships maintained, the process of cooperating to solve conflict can actually improve them. The outcome of cooperating is that everyone involved in the conflict ends up feeling that they got more of what they needed than they had to give up. The resolution is mutually acceptable. Of the five conflict strategies, this is the most time-consuming, but usually the most worthwhile.

The Teambuilt Approach to Conflict

To be successful, teams need to use a mix of approaches, depending on the type of conflict to be resolved and the circumstances. There are, however, some guidelines and techniques that can help teams minimize the negative consequences of conflict and maximize the outcomes.

Teach Team Members to Be Better Conflict Resolvers. Make sure all team members understand the different approaches available and when each is appropriate.

Take a Working Approach to Conflict. Conflict is like the turbulence pilots and air travelers experience en route to their destinations. When pilots encounter turbulence, they adjust their flight paths. They may go over, under, or around the turbulence, but unless the turbulence is dangerously severe, they continue moving toward their destinations. The team's destination is determined by its vision. Teams know that they need to deal with conflicts that arise, but that can be done en route. I call this the working approach to conflict: team members work through conflicts while progressing toward the team vision. They stay focused on the team vision rather than becoming sidetracked by the conflict; only the most severe conflict should be able to interrupt the team's progress.

Agree as a Team How You'll Approach Conflict. Encourage team members to use this three-step approach to conflict. If a team member senses a conflict with another member, the first step is to approach that member. This technique is called *diplomatic confrontation.* Team members should agree not to involve third parties without first making an attempt to work thought the conflict themselves.

If they are unable to resolve the problem, the second step is *mediation.* Mediation occurs when the parties involved in the conflict present their sides of the story to a third party who recommends a solution. Mediation is not binding. It is up to the people involved to implement the recommended solution, but they can choose to modify it, or do something completely different. One approach to mediation is to agree in advance to implement whatever solution the mediator suggests. The mediator can be any other team member who isn't personally involved in the conflict—but often it is the job of the team leader.

If mediation is unsuccessful, the third step is *arbitration.* Arbitration occurs when a third party of authority imposes a solution because those involved in the conflict were unable or unwilling to resolve the situation themselves.

Diplomatic Confrontation in Action

When people describe their approach to conflict, frequently they say they have to confront someone. Although this is a common approach to dealing with problems, it is flawed from the onset because very few people like to be confronted.

You don't check your calendar in the morning to see how many confrontations you have scheduled. And when was the last time you found yourself thinking, "Great! I've got an opening at 1:30. If I hurry, maybe I can schedule another confrontation for then." More likely, you will try to avoid—or at least postpone—a personal confrontation as long as possible. Confronting people is an ineffective strategy.

Picture this situation: you're checking into a hotel. As you wait in line, you overhear a heated conversation between the desk clerk and the guest in front of you. It seems the guest had a reservation but the hotel can't find it—and there are no more rooms.

How does the guest without a room react? He confronts the clerk, verbally abusing and maybe even threatening him. But this is dumb behavior because the only person who can give him a key to a room is the desk clerk. Attacking turns the clerk into an opponent, rather than an ally.

Diplomatic confrontation doesn't attack the desk clerk, it confronts the problem. The conversation might go something like this: "I understand that you didn't personally lose my reservation. I'm certainly not mad at you but I'm frustrated by the situation. I've had a reservation for at least two months and I need your help." This approach doesn't guarantee you'll get a room, but it increases the likelihood of a positive outcome. By confronting problems instead of people, you'll find people more willing to help you solve the problems.

Diplomatic confrontation can be summarized succinctly:

Don't confront people, confront problems.

Team members need to learn how to confront diplomatically because it allows them to maintain positive relationships by being soft on the person but tough on the problem.

Admittedly, there are times when it is more fun to confront people. It feels good to attack someone when we're upset. But ultimately, like the hotel guest, you must choose: Do you want to feel good, or do you want a key to solve your problem?

PLAYING GAMES FOR FUN AND PROFIT

One of the most frequent questions I'm asked is, "What are some activities we can use at team meetings and retreats to help build teamwork?"

Games are an excellent training device because they let team members experience a concept rather than simply hear about it. Children don't learn to ride a bike by listening to the instructions adults provide. The real learning is when they apply what they've been told. Likewise, teamwork concepts are abstract until experienced. Games enhance the learning experience by involving more of the senses and providing participants with personal insights that would be difficult to achieve through passive training.

Sports teams get to practice during the off season. Why not think of games as a form of practice for your own team?

Another reason for playing games: it encourages interaction among team members in a nonthreatening way. Some people find it difficult to ask people they don't know for help, even if they're on the same team. Personal interaction outside a work setting makes it easier for team members to cooperate on team projects. While the intent of a team game may be serious, the game isn't. Interacting in an environment of "antiseriousness" helps team members get to know each other better.

Finally, playing games strips away pretensions. As a speaker and seminar leader, I often put my audiences into small groups for exercises and discussions. But I have to admit that I personally hate participating in group exercises. For me, it is easier to learn by listening than by interacting with other people. I make this confession because, despite my hesitation, I always give in and participate in the exercise I'm asked to do. And once the exercise is over, I'm always glad I participated. Personal experience has taught me that it is easy to maintain barriers and facades with others, and games are one of the most effective techniques for breaking through.

Here are three fun games that teach some important teambuilt concepts.

Cooperative Volleyball

The first game is a variation of a familiar sport. It's called "Cooperative Volleyball" and it's very easy to play. The only props required are a volleyball and net. The game is identical to regular volleyball except in scoring and rotation. The objective is to keep the ball in the air. The score is based on the number of volleys before the ball hits the ground. Rotation includes changing sides of the net, not just positions. The type of rotation you choose is not critical as long as players rotate across sides.

Cooperative volleyball redirects competitiveness. The "opponent" is past performance rather than the players on the other side of the net. The goal is to improve performance by completing more successful volleys each serve. Players may initially be skeptical, but should soon find the game challenging in a manner that is very different from past experience.

The Human Knot

The second game, "The Human Knot," is also relatively easy because it requires no props.

Begin by asking for 6 to 10 volunteers. Ask them to form a circle. Then to make the game more interesting, ask every other person to face outward. The next step is critical: each player must join hands with two others, but neither can be on either side. In other words, the knot is formed by joining hands with people who are not next to you.

The objective of this game is to untie the knot without dropping hands. It's permissible to change holds or pivot hand positions, but players can't release and then rejoin their hands to untie the knot.

Once in progress, the game appears to be a form of mutant disco dancing. Players should be comfortable moving around each other in very close contact. Since this is a physical exercise that involves stepping over and moving under other players, short skirts and tight clothing are not advised. (For any game, members should be encouraged to participate, but forced participation is not a good idea.)

This game is usually best played with a time limit; 10 minutes works well. Much longer and the action begins to lag. Be forewarned: some human knots cannot be untied.

Processing the Game

The following questions can be discussed with both participants and others who observed the game; observers share often some valuable insights.

Did Someone Take Charge or Was It More of a Participative Effort? Often an informal leader quickly emerges. They are allowed to suggest or direct, but only for a while. Then they are displaced as leaders if their suggestions and directions haven't brought the team closer to a solution. Sometimes the groups acts on input from anyone who offers it. Total participation can result in total chaos. Perhaps a combination of autocratic and participative approaches were used. Draw out lessons based on which approach the team took and how well it worked.

When Was Feedback Helpful? When Was It Not Helpful? What Could Have Been Done to Improve Communication Between Players? The human knot hinges on players' abilities not just to come up with good ideas but to communicate them effectively. That often means convincing others to try something they don't think will work. Talk about the feedback that helped untie the knot—what worked and what didn't.

How Does It Feel to Be Dependent on Other People to Untie the

Knot and to Solve a Problem? Most of us are used to working alone and solving our own problems. This forced interdependency is an important illustration of teamwork.

What Should You Do When Nothing Has Worked? How Long Should You Play Before Giving Up? Ask players if they think all problems (knots) can be solved. One option available to players is to cheat. In games, cheating means breaking the rules. But in real-life teamwork, cheating doesn't have to mean doing something wrong or unethical. It could mean working outside the boundaries that have confined team success in the past. (See Chapter 12, "Taking the Team Through Tough Times.")

If You Were Going to Coach Another Team on How to Play the Human Knot, What Would You Tell Them? Have players suggest guidelines or shortcuts that could be passed on to help future players succeed more quickly.

Variations

There are two variations that can be used to make the human knot more challenging. The first is to request that players not talk. Eliminating verbal feedback adds an interesting twist. The second variation is to blindfold players. This increases the need for accurate feedback. (For those who really like to stack the odds, combine the two variations.)

The River of Boiling Oil

The third game is called "The River of Boiling Oil." Imagine this scenario: you and your team are hiking in a wilderness area when you become lost. It is beginning to get dark and you must make it back before nightfall. You come upon the dreaded River of Boiling Oil and realize that the only way to make it back in time is to cross the dangerous river.

As you and your team contemplate the River of Boiling Oil, you realize that anyone who falls in will be fried instantly. Crossing the river requires magical french fries. Magical french fries float. By placing them in the River of Boiling Oil, you and your team members can go from fry to fry to eventually cross the river.

Lucky for you, you're carrying a number of these magical french fries in your backpacks. Strangely enough, they look just like 2' × 4' boards that have been cut in various lengths from 6" to 24". (You can get up to six people on a board that's 24" long.) Prior to playing the game, go to a local lumberyard or building store and stock up on magical fries.

The river should be roughly two volleyball courts wide. The team starts on one side of the imaginery River of Boiling Oil. Each member is equipped with one magical fry to place in the river. Once members are in the river, they must stay on the fries. If they fall off, they must go back to the beginning point on the riverbank.

Variations
There are a number of interesting variations you can add to this exercise. The first is "the sinking magical french fries." How does a magical fry sink? The game facilitator removes it. If the team is crossing too easily, you can start removing their resources. When somebody places a magical french fry, pick it up. A word of warning: some team members have been known to become violent when their fry is removed.

Another variation is to have a team member remove magical french fries. You might wonder why you would want to do that. In real life, management must often remove resources from the team. You can create team empathy for how tough these resource allocation decisions are by putting team members in management's role. The game simulates not only how it feels when resources are diminished, but what it is like to be the person who allocates resources.

If you find that your team is not making it across the River of Boiling Oil, you can narrow the distance to make it a little bit easier. After they have made it to the other side, process what they experienced by discussing these questions.

How Did You Feel When Someone Fell In? Teams often become frustrated with a team member who is not performing, or who is holding the team back. Is your team sufficiently patient and encouraging with team members when this occurs? How do team members accept responsibility for their own failures? Are they able to rebound quickly?

How Did You React When Resources Were Removed? Teams should be able to move quickly from grumbling and complaining to taking constructive action.

How Were You Able to Accomplish Your Objective with Limited Resources? What Strategies Did the Team Develop to Deal with the Diminished Resources? Removing magical fries requires players to work more carefully at sharing the remaining fries. They may need to increase physical contact to keep from falling off and make it across the river. Are team members willing to do what's necessary—and maybe uncomfortable—to get the job done?

How Do You Know When There Are Too Few Resources? There is a point where, if you remove enough french fries, it doesn't matter how dedicated or skilled the team is, they're not going to be able to make it across.

What Should You Do When There Are Too Few Resources? This question identifies how a team should respond once they become convinced that lack of resources is a limitation which cannot be successfully overcome.

How Did It Feel to Be Responsible for Cutting Back on Resources and How Did You Decide Which Resources to Remove? Ask this only if you decided to use the variation where one of the team members removed the magical french fries.

9

STEP 4:
COMMUNICATE

*"The greatest illusion about communication
is the belief that it has been accomplished."*
George Bernard Shaw

According to novelist Carlos Fuentes, the greatest crisis facing modern civilization will be transforming information into structured knowledge. If we're going to make information useful in an overcommunicated world, we have to find a way to give facts and figures context and meaning for team members.

Management guru Peter Drucker says that for an organization to be information-based it doesn't necessarily need to take advantage of advanced information technology. It only requires that everyone in the organization ask one central question:

Who needs what information, when, and where?

I touched on the some of the qualities of effective interpersonal communication in the section on building strong team relationships. Now let's examine two more important qualities of team communication: *accuracy* and *honesty*.

Accuracy

Accuracy is the logical component of team communication. It means making sure that the information team members send and receive is valid when compared to actual experience.

What is the most dangerous location in your organization? The toxic waste disposal site? The shop floor? The fork lift? The loading dock? Any of those places poses a safety hazard, but probably the most dangerous place is behind a desk. A desk is an information distortion filter. Usually when verbal or written information crosses a desktop, it mutates. It tends to get embellished, edited, twisted, and misinterpreted. The best way to ensure accurate information is to go to the source and get close to the people who are making it happen—or having it happen to them. This is especially important for team leadership.

MBWA—"Management By Wandering Around"—became a familiar acronym when Tom Peters and Bob Waterman released their book *In Search of Excellence.* To use Peters's words, they'd struck "a blinding flash of the obvious." As they studied excellent companies, they found that effective managers and leaders wander a lot. To be informed means to be given information. Those who practice MBWA are accurately informed because they're "out there"—not trying to manage from behind an information distortion filter.

One factor that makes teamwork work is that all members have the opportunity to share their experiences from "out there." Decisions are based on better information because it comes from the people on the front lines.

But what about the information that team members are given? If they are to make good decisions, teams must be given more and better information than most organizations have traditionally been willing to provide. Giving more and better information to team members not only improves the quality of their decisions, it improves their commitment to the decision. Increasing availability of information is a trust issue as much as a performance issue.

Does this mean disclosing all organizational information to team members? Definitely not. It means making available *relevant information*—information the team believes it needs. Offer to provide whatever information they believe is necessary for their success. (Confidential employee files are an exception, for obvious reasons.) Team members can always "edit down" information they don't need, but they can't "edit up"—that is, fill in missing information they don't have. To truly teambuild, err on the side of too much rather than too little.

Let's distinguish between information organizations feel is "confidential" and what is really more often "uncomfortable." One business owner who decided to make complete financial information available to all employees found that his managers were uncomfortable with this because it meant employees would know their salaries. The owner's conclusion: if managers are uncomfortable about employees knowing what they're paid, *maybe it's because they know they can't prove they're really earning their pay.*

Afraid to impart proprietary information? Emphasize to team members that the information is confidential. If they feel any ownership or pride in their organization, you can be assured that they will respect the sensitivity of the information they're given. If they don't, you've got an even larger problem to deal with. When it comes to giving team members information,

Lack is worse than leaks.

Honesty

Honesty is the emotional component of team communication. Few things are more time-consuming and energy-draining than hidden agendas and unexpressed feelings.

131

Norm Lawson is vice president of sales for Dreyer's Grand Ice Cream, a company that has enjoyed success over the past 15 years because of teamwork. Dreyer's is known for its corporate culture of openness and camaraderie, a tone that is set by the seven officers of the Executive Committee. Lawson says, "The seven officers are a team. However, they fight, fuss, and fume over business issues and decisions, but never get personal about the differences of opinion they might have. The teamwork is so ingrained at Dreyer's that the seven of us cross over into one another's departments without any anger or misunderstandings. There is only one rule—we don't give orders or direction to someone in another department. We just communicate and share a point of view."

Dreyer's has achieved something that is uncommon at any level in corporate America, but even more amazing among upper-level managers: honest communication. As simplistic as it sounds, by focusing on "sharing a point of view," the executive team can move more quickly and honestly. Each team member knows what the others are feeling, and there's no need to worry about facades and issues that will come up later after action is taken.

THE INFO MODEL

All team communication should be accurate and honest. To help you focus your team communications, try my INFO model: *Ideas, News, Feedback,* and *Outcomes.*

Ideas: The Art of Improving

The first component of INFO team communication is *ideas* for innovating and improving. An old saying comes to mind:

Inch by inch, life's a cinch. Yard by yard, life is hard.

Making significant gains in any one area of your team's or organization's performance is difficult. In America, we value big gains—we have a "home-run mentality" that says when you step up to the plate, you should try to hit the ball out of the park. The problem with this approach is that home-run hitters tend to strike out a lot. There's nothing wrong with trying to hit home runs, but there are other ways to score. The Japanese have figured out another way: they look at big improvements as the sum of many tiny improvements. The word for their approach is. *kaizen,* which means "continuous improvement involving everyone."

McDonald's has long dominated the $55-billion-plus fast food industry. CEO Michael Quinlan says the secret to McDonald's' success is that they are never content with the way things are. This approach requires taking a team or organization apart, nut by nut, bolt by bolt, task by task, and asking the fundamental question, "How can we do it just a little bit better?" That's the attitude that drives team kaizen—continuous improvement involving everybody.

Incentives for Ideas
Present a "Mistake of the Month Award." Not a form of humiliation, this award is legitimate recognition of the people on your team who are trying new things. How can we encourage people to try new things and experiment with new ideas if we only reward the ones that succeed? Whenever team members feel that mistakes will be punished, they will forgo any risk likely to incur punishment. By recognizing the attempt rather than the outcome, the Mistake of the Month Award proves that it's OK to fail if you're trying something new.

At a well-known computer company there was a product manager who attempted a daring new launch that bombed to the tune of $5 million. The story goes that after the dust had settled from this marketing fiasco, the founder and then CEO called the product manager into his office. Head hung low and hands in his pockets, the manager respectfully said, "I suppose you expect my resignation, sir." The great man stared back and said, "Are you kidding me? I just spent $5 million educating you!"

Chances are pretty good that this exchange transformed the failed product manager into one of the most innovative people at the company—if he applied what he learned from his $5 million education. Whether or not that story is true, it makes a powerful point:

When it comes to trying something new, reward the attempt, not just the outcome.

Here's a fun way to create a Mistake of the Month Award. Varnish some turkey feathers, then stick them to a piece of plywood, and you've got a rotating plaque. Present the award at a team meeting and ask the recipient to explain what he or she was attempting, what happened, and most importantly, what was learned from the attempt. End the presentation by reminding team members that you won't shoot them for making mistakes, but you might shoot them for never trying anything new.

Create Idea Quotas. Ask team members to come up with at least one new idea each week. Encourage them to visit other businesses, read books and trade publications, and look for new ways of doing old things better. Idea quotas encourage people to come up with ideas on a regular basis. Otherwise, team members are too busy to think creatively. This creative exercise could move you light years ahead of your competitors.

LaRosa's is a family-style Italian restaurant chain in Cincinnati. Periodically they load up the company van with their management team and go to dinner at an excellent restaurant somewhere in the tri-state area. They come back with literally a van-load of ideas they've learned from observing during their field trip.

You may be in an industry where showing up at your competitor's door for a tour would not be hospitably received. No problem—visit an organization outside your industry and benefit from *the displacement concept.* If you only do what everybody else in your industry is doing, you'll never be truly innovative but only emulative. Find ideas outside your industry and become the first to apply them in yours, and you'll have an edge.

Pay for Non-Job-Related Seminars and Classes. There are two kinds of information team members can use. The first is *logistical information.* Logistical information has a known use. For example, if your team is embarking on a quality program and you send machine operators to a seminar on statistical process control, they can immediately use the information when they return.

But there's another kind of information important to teamwork. *Nutrient information* is the seedbed for innovation and improvement. Nutrient information has little or no immediate known use, but over time, team members find creative application for the ideas derived.

Attending seminars and classes that are not job-related provides nutrient information. A class on the history of great battles might provide excellent fodder for a marketing team. An overview of general systems theory could provide new insights for a manufacturing team. Paying for team members to periodically attend non-job-related seminars or classes provides a richer environment of nutrient information that will allow them to think more innovatively.

Present a Weekly Challenge. This concept can be used with individuals or the entire group. One week before the team meeting, assign a current problem or challenge to one or more members. Ask them to come up with at least three solutions to present at the meeting. Then use their recommendations as a springboard for discussion and action.

To make this concept a group activity, write the weekly challenge on a large sheet of paper that you post in a common area. Ask team members to write their ideas and comments on the paper.

Some teams ask members to maintain a notebook. At the team meeting, they discuss a challenge that they're all going to be thinking about before the next meeting. Then at the next meeting, they synthesize ideas and strategize their action plan.

The weekly challenge is a means of reminding your team to continually look for solutions to problems and challenges.

Call a Brainstorming Break. You're probably familiar with brainstorming: a problem is identified and everyone in the session suggests ideas. No idea is evaluated until a large quantity have been generated. Then they are considered, eliminated, and combined to form a workable solution.

During a lull time, or to relieve the stress of a hectic period, call a quick break. Ask team members to join you for 15 minutes in your office or a nearby meeting room. If they're not already familiar with brainstorming, briefly explain the concept. Then use the balance of time to brainstorm a relevant topic. At the end of the session, thank the team for their help. Now they can return to their work, refreshed from the mental break.

Form Superteams for Innovation. The regional office of a long-distance company in my area created a superteam. It was a cross-functional team that included one representative from every department in their organization. They met once a month for breakfast and brainstormed across departmental boundaries. These sessions generated valuable ideas for organizational improvement, helped break down territorial boundaries, and expedited interdepartmental teamwork.

News

The N in INFO stands for *news.* If team members don't know what's going on in their company, they tend to make up their own news based on hearsay and gossip. Sharing informal information about the team and organization can be troublesome, if it's not handled properly. Team members need to be able to differentiate between news and gossip before sharing their thoughts.

Several years ago a friend who's a psychotherapist shared an idea that provides a practical distinction between news and gossip. During group counseling sessions for clients, she's found that in any small group, there is almost always one person with the potential to dominate—they seem to talk just to hear themselves talk. To prevent this, at the beginning of the session she lays down a ground rule: "Before you say anything, ask yourself, 'Is what I'm about to say for *my* benefit or for the *group's* benefit?' If it doesn't benefit the group, withhold the comment."

A similar practice can be used at team meetings: news is information that builds relationships; gossip is information that tears them down. Information that team members can't use to build relationships or improve performance most likely falls into the category of gossip and should be withheld.

The Team Grapevine: Wine or Whine?

The grapevine exists. There will always be a rumor mill where you work, so use it to make fine wine. Use the grapevine to your advantage by fueling it with good news. Share success stories, team member accomplishments, external recognition from customers or the media, and any other positive news you have about the organization.

Research in this area suggests that about 10 percent of the people in any organization actively pass information back and forth—they are the grapevine. Fifty percent of the people in any organization are recipients of that information. But about 30 percent to 40 percent don't use the grapevine to either pass or receive information. So if you fuel the grapevine with good news stories, you'll set a positive agenda for at least 60 percent of the people in your organization.

Powerful Team Meetings

The formal setting for sharing news and other important information is the team meeting. Meetings in general have a deservedly bad reputation for at least three reasons: 1) they last too long, 2) they're boring, and 3) they waste people's time. (In one survey, executives said that one out of every three meetings they attend each week is a complete waste of their time.) To ensure powerful team meetings, make them quick, make them interesting, and make sure they are a good investment of time.

Deciding how often your team should meet depends on two things: 1) how much new information needs to be shared and 2) how much interaction team members have each week. Team meetings become increasingly important when you've got team members who work in the field, in different facilities, or on different shifts. It's very difficult to develop a sense of camaraderie and interdependence with someone you never see.

As a general rule, teams should meet at least once a month. Once every two weeks is a good idea, and weekly may be necessary for some teams.

The Six Components of Powerful Team Meetings

Accomplishments and Blunders. You can begin the team meeting with a short review of accomplishments and blunders. (Sometimes referred to as "roses and onions.") This is a recap of what the team has done right and what the team has done, well . . . not so right.

To get the discussion started, ask a couple of questions at the beginning of each meeting. "What has happened since the last team meeting that you are most proud of?" This gives people a chance to share some good news. The focus should be on team accomplishments; individual recognition will come later. The other question is, "What has happened since the last team meeting that you want to make sure doesn't happen again?" Remind team members not to place blame but to bring up areas where mistakes need to be avoided and performance improved. Accomplishments can be teamwide or individual, but blunders should never be attributed to an individual in a meeting setting. Stick to areas where the team needs to do better.

Follow-up. The second component is follow-up from your last team meeting. This is the time to review the action plan the team developed. Specific tasks were assigned. Ask those responsible for an update on their progress.

Make sure that what was discussed at the last meeting is getting done.

Problem Solving and Planning. The first two components shouldn't take long, maybe 5 to 10 minutes. The third component is a discussion of what needs to be done, followed by a completed action plan. Discussing problems as a team can potentially turn your meeting into a complaint session. Here's how to avoid that: Discuss a problem long enough to identify its cause. Once that's accomplished, address three questions: 1) What needs to be done? 2) Who is willing to do it? 3) What resources will it take? This keeps the focus on action rather than on complaining.

Recognition. The fourth component is recognition. Time should be set aside for acknowledging and rewarding the achievements of individual team members. Here's an important secret team leaders should know about recognition:

Over time, every team member should be recognized for something.

Don't try to recognize everybody at each team meeting. Team members will see it as a gimmick. The point is to find something about every member that can be recognized, not every time the team meets, but over time so that nobody feels they aren't contributing. With some team members, this may mean you'll have to search long and hard to find something worth recognizing.

Inexpensive software programs that allow you to turn your personal computer into a certificate maker are readily available. Be imaginative in creating certificates to recognize the varied and unusual contributions team members make. Have some fun doing it. For example, if you've just come through a particularly difficult period, recognize someone with a "Mr. or Ms. Positive Attitude" certificate. If a team member has recently put in long hours to complete a project, print up a "We hope your family still recognizes you!" certificate. It isn't the cost of the certificate that team members appreciate, it's the fact that someone took time to notice and appreciate what they've done.

Professional Development. This is an important time for professional enrichment and education. The team meeting will be more interesting if you take advantage of different approaches. There are a number of short but effective instructional tools you can use. Here are a few pointers.

If you don't have time to show an entire training video, show a 10- to 15-minute excerpt. The same can be done with an instructional audio cassette. Isolate an audio or video segment that addresses a timely topic for the team. Write down some of the most important ideas and quotes and have them typed into a summary that can be distributed at the end of the professional development section. You could also prepare two or three questions based on the excerpt and use them as a springboard for discussion after viewing or listening. Make sure team members know the complete programs are available from the team resource center.

Invite a guest speaker to present. A professional speaker is an option, but since time is limited at most team meetings, there may be a better alternative. How about a customer who is delighted with the service your team's been providing? Or an unhappy customer, whom you invite to talk about ways to make service better? Consider asking someone from another department to make a short presentation on what their group does, how it affects your team, and what they need from you to increase organizational effectiveness. Periodically invite someone from upper management to give a "state of the company" presentation.

If you use a presenter, clarify in advance what you'd like the speaker to address and how much time you've allotted. If necessary, work with the speaker to make sure the presentation is interesting and powerful. Two things can destroy the effectiveness of this portion of your meeting: a speaker who takes too long, or a presentation that isn't relevant or interesting.

General Announcements. The final few minutes of the meeting should be reserved for general announcements. To prevent this from becoming tedious, try printing detailed general information and distributing it before the announcements. Include the name and phone extension of someone to call if there are questions not covered in the printed material. Then you can refer team members to the printed information as you quickly make the verbal announcements.

To keep interest—and attendance—high, plan a *mystery announcement* for the end of every meeting. Use teasers such as "Find out who just set a new company record," or "At the next meeting we will announce a commitment management has just made that will revolutionize our phone systems."

The core of any team meeting is problem solving and planning. Carefully control the time spent on the other five elements to maximize the time spent here. Experiment with the format. You may find that a different order works better for you. Just remember to keep the team meeting lively and focused on providing information the team can use to improve performance.

Any action planning you have done at the team meeting should be typed and distributed immediately. Make sure someone is responsible for recording accurate notes for this purpose.

One of the ways you can develop leadership among your team is to rotate responsibility for planning and executing team meetings. Make sure every team member gets a chance to be in charge of a meeting.

If you aren't comfortable doing that, appoint one person to work on the professional development portion. Each team meeting gives you a chance to involve members in building their organizational and leadership skills.

Dealing with Nonparticipation

Sometimes you have team members who won't or don't participate. Dealing with nonparticipation isn't as hard as you might believe. Two reasons why people don't participate is that they aren't prepared or don't want to appear foolish. When an issue is raised, they may want to think it through before voicing their opinions.

One solution is to delegate participation well in advance of the meeting. Identify a nonparticipating team member and ask her for help. Tell her what is going to be discussed and asked her to be prepared to share her opinion. To make it easier, encourage advance discussion with other team members to find out what they think as well. That way, her comments at the meeting will represent the views of others as well. This team member is less likely to feel foolish if she knows in advance what others are thinking. Make sure this member knows she will be expected to present at the team meeting, and give her sufficient time to be ready. Using this rather formal approach will draw in people who otherwise might not get involved. Once they've presented formally, they should be less afraid to get involved informally at future meetings.

Feedback

The third component of the INFO model is *feedback.* Any information that can be used to improve performance is feedback. But feedback and constructive criticism are not synonymous:

"Constructive criticism" is a myth.

To construct means to build. To criticize means to tear down. It doesn't make sense to try to build people by tearing them down. The phrase "constructive criticism" elicits a negative response from most people because they know it's a weak attempt to soften the criticism that is about to be leveled at them.

Occasionally someone will approach me at the end of one of my programs and ask, "Would you like a little constructive criticism?" My response is always, "No, thank you." I then explain that I will be glad to listen to ideas on how my presentation performance could be improved. But I want the person to focus his remarks on what I did, not on me.

There is a significant difference between criticism and feedback. Criticism focuses on the person. Feedback focuses on the performance. Making me feel bad about who I am will not help me improve what I do. So, if I haven't made my opinion clear: *stop criticizing, constructively or otherwise.* It seldom accomplishes the intended result.

Feedback is another example of the important differences between a work group and a team. In a work group, feedback only moves down. For this feedback to be accepted and taken seriously, it must come from someone "higher up" in the organization, typically the manager or supervisor.

> *In a team, feedback should be accepted from anyone*
> *who can provide it.*

If the information offered is useful for improving an individual's performance, it shouldn't make any difference who provides it—the team leader, a fellow team member, or even someone lower in the organizational hierarchy. For many team members, receiving feedback on their performance from someone who isn't their formal boss will be a new experience. It may be even more difficult for them to give performance feedback to others. Team leadership must be willing to demonstrate an openness to this multidirectional feedback if the idea is to work. Also, team members should be taught how to give valid feedback.

Feedback Focuses on What Was Done Rather than Who Did It. Most of us started getting constructive criticism long before we entered the work world. The role models we had—parents and peers—weren't very good at providing feedback.

It's always sad to hear an adult tell a small child, "You're a little pig." But I've never seen a pig-child. None of my friends' kids have bristly hair all over their bodies, long snouts, or curly tails. Consider this: To have a piggy child, you must be a piggy parent! Thankfully, there are no piggy parents or piggy kids. So what causes an adult to call a child a little pig? Usually it's something the child did or didn't do—spilled a glass of milk or left toys on the floor.

Directing harsh remarks at the child makes the child think there is something wrong with him (If I'm a pig, then spilling milk and making a mess is appropriate behavior). Attacking another person's self-esteem is an ineffective way to get him or her to improve performance or behavior. The better alternative is to focus on behavior—what the person did.

Thus the message to the child becomes, "Please pick up your toys.

It's not good to leave them lying on the floor." The child now knows what to do to improve his behavior, and doesn't feel there is anything wrong with him.

It may seem odd to use this example in a book about teamwork. I'm not suggesting we treat adults in a childlike manner, but there is much to be gained by understanding how and what we learned as kids, for a lot of that stuff followed us into adulthood.

There are two types of feedback: *corrective* and *improvement.*

The message of corrective feedback is *this is what should not be done or should be done differently.* When giving corrective feedback, it's helpful to involve the receiver. After explaining what happened and the resulting situation, ask the other person, "What could you have done to improve the outcome?"

Active learning is more effective than passive learning, as long as the other person doesn't think your question is condescending. Getting his or her ideas will provide additional information that may improve the corrective feedback you'll then offer.

The message of improvement feedback is *this is what could be done to make the outcome even better.* In this situation, the receiver has done an acceptable job, but you've noticed something that would either make it easier for the person next time or would improve or enhance the results.

When giving improvement feedback, it helps to preface the feedback with a question: "Have you considered . . . ?" Maybe the other person has already thought about what you're going to say and has reached a different conclusion. Giving improvement feedback can create the impression that you don't believe the other person is as knowledgeable or skilled as you are. Whether or not that is the case, the person will be more receptive to your suggestion if you've given him the benefit of the doubt.

Feedback Should Be Instructive Rather than Irritating. Effective feedback has got to give people information they can use—that's instruction. If all you succeed in doing is making them angry or frustrated, that's irritating.

Vague statements such as "Give better customer service," or "Improve your attitude," or "Be more patient" are irritating because they give no specific instruction about what needs to be done.

To convert vague statements into instructive feedback, use the rule of OMB: Observable, Measurable Behavior. By giving feedback in terms of observable, measurable behavior, the receiver will know exactly what needs to be done to improve.

Consider the statement, "Give better customer service." What observable, measurable behaviors define "better customer service"? Let's assume the crux of the problem is that the team member is giving incomplete or inaccurate information. Using OMB, the feedback becomes, "When you answer customers' questions, be sure the information is correct. You may need to double check the information with another department. If that's the case, arrange to call them back. At the end of the conversation, ask if they have all the information they need." That feedback is specific enough to be instructional.

Wait for the teachable moment. The time when the feedback is most helpful to the receiver. It may not be the time when it is most convenient for the person who wants to give it.

The wrong time to give feedback is when you are emotionally involved in the situation. If a team member has disappointed and you feel the need to "get it off your chest," no one will benefit much from the feedback. The teachable moment is usually when the giver is *objective* and the receiver is *ready to utilize it.*

There's an inventory concept called "Just-In-Time" that can be adapted to feedback. To the degree possible, give feedback on a person's performance whenever he's about to repeat that performance. With the feedback fresh in mind, a person can readily apply it to the task at hand. (Not all behavior is predictable enough or significant enough for this approach.)

Outcomes

The final component of the INFO model is *outcomes.* Whenever we communicate, we create an outcome. The outcome will be a change in the way the team member thinks, feels, or acts. The success of any communication should be evaluated on the basis of whether it created the intended result. When we haven't designed our communication to elicit a certain outcome, we often get an unintended one. It is the difference between communicating by design versus communicating by default.

Unclear communication creates unclear outcomes.

In Chapter 5, "Beyond Goal Setting," I suggested that a goal could easily be clarified by explaining five things to your team: what, how much, how well, by when, and for whom. Those factors can also be used to ensure that team members know exactly what we'd like when we communicate with them.

The Obstacles to Outcomes

If communicating outcomes is as simple as clarifying those five factors, what so often prevents us from getting the outcomes we desire? There are several common barriers. The first is *ignoring the emotions created by the messages we send.*

The emotions we create when we communicate are just as important as the messages we send. If we make team members defensive, they will find it hard to listen or agree. If we offend them, they will resist what we tell them—even if it's valid. Yet the busier we become, the less attention most of us pay to the emotional aspect of our communications.

Somebody once said that diplomacy is the ability to tell a person to take a hike and make them look forward to the trip. There is wisdom in that humor.

> *You can't always tell team members what they want to hear, but you can almost always tell them in such a way that they'll be willing to listen.*

The key to tact and diplomacy is being sensitive to the way people feel instead of focusing exclusively on the information we send.

The second barrier affects us as listeners. It is *assuming you know when you don't.* The human mind can make sense out of limited information. This is a wonderful ability, but it can also be a curse when we draw the wrong conclusions because we didn't consider all the information. As soon as we think we know what the other person means, we tend to stop listening—even though the person may still be talking. Hence the phrase "jumping to conclusions." Overcoming this barrier requires the discipline to hear people out and ask questions to try to truly understand what they mean.

The third barrier is related to assumption as well. When we assume the listener knows something he doesn't, we've just been affected by *the COIK fallacy*—Clear Only If Known. If you ask a new team member to "prepare a bid in the standard format," you assume the person knows what the standard format is. Unless you are reasonably certain that is the case, COIK can be avoided by asking what the person knows about the standard format and then explaining the rest.

It seems ludicrous that people wouldn't just tell us that they don't know what we're talking about. Yet experience shows that this happens all the time. The most common reasons: they don't know that they don't know or they are too intimidated to admit they don't know.

The fourth barrier, which I call *the clairvoyance trap*, is illustrated in this story I heard from an employee in Canton, Ohio. The employee had turned in a project to his manager. The manager reviewed it and said the project was unsatisfactory. The employee asked what the manager wanted instead. His reply: "I'm not sure, but this isn't it." The employee asked what he should do. I suggested that he seek psychiatric counseling for his boss.

Have you ever had another person get angry at you for not giving him what you didn't know he wanted? When you asked why, his response was, "You should have known. If you a) understood the situation, b) thought about it, or c) cared for me, you would have known without my asking."

The clairvoyance trap is expecting another team member to be able to read your mind. Maybe this comes from a twisted sense that we shouldn't ask for things. The reality is that it isn't nice to demand, but there's usually nothing wrong with asking.

> *If you're not getting what you need to make the*
> *relationship work, ask for it.*

This is a no-risk strategy. The worst thing that will happen is that you won't get what you asked for—but you weren't getting it to begin with. At least by asking you know the other person is clear about what you need, and choosing not to cooperate.

COMMUNICATING IDEAS

There are 279 words in the 10 Commandments. If Moses (with God's help) could codify all moral law in 279 words, a team should be able to keep most written communication to one page or less. Memos longer than one page often waste the time of the writer and the reader.

When presenting an idea, in writing or verbally, here's a format that can keep the presentation concise and yet effective. The format is PEPI:

Proposal
Evidence
Plan
Ideas

The proposal is a one-sentence statement of the main idea. Keeping it to one sentence helps the presenter refine the message so that it is arrow-tip sharp.

Evidence is the data that support the idea. The objective is to persuade the reader or listener that the proposal is worthwhile and valid.

The plan is a mini-action plan that explains what should be done and who should do it.

The ideas portion is actually a question: "You now know what I'm proposing . . . any ideas?" This involves the reader or listener in a response that may even improve the original idea.

10

STEP 5: MOTIVATE

USING REWARDS AND RECOGNITION TO PRODUCE RESULTS

Motivation is about getting people to do what you want. It's important to understand the corollary—why team members *don't* do what you want them to do. No matter how many reasons you might list, all can be grouped into five simple categories that will help you identify the problem and analyze potential solutions.

Why Don't Team Members Do What They're Supposed To?

The major reason we don't get the behavior we want from people is that *they don't know what it is they're supposed to do.* This is a communication problem and that's why clarifying outcomes is so important.

The second reason they fail: they know what they're supposed to do, but *they don't know how to do it.* This is a training problem. That's why strategic anticipation—preceding every increase in responsibility with the appropriate training—is essential.

The third reason why team members don't do what you want

them to do is that *they aren't capable of doing it.* This is a selection problem that results when team members are put in situations which are over their heads. If you have a team member who sincerely wants to perform, is willing to take the necessary training, but then still can't master the task, consider the problem to be ability. In other words, the person simply can't do what it is you're asking.

The fourth reason why people don't produce the results you expect is probably the least likely in most workplaces: they know what to do, how to do it, they're capable of doing it, but *they refuse to do it.* This is an insubordination problem that, in its extreme form, should lead to removal.

The fifth and most important reason people don't do what we expect is that *they don't have a reason why they should do it.* This is a motivation problem. Motivation is providing people with a motive for action, giving them a reason that makes sense to them.

BEYOND THE QUICK FIX: FUNDAMENTALS OF MOTIVATION

Motivation has never been difficult in traditional work groups where there is a "boss." With clear-cut authority, the boss can mandate "It's my way or the highway." The quick fix in American business has always been compliance and intimidation: "Just do it." That approach elicits an equally childlike response: "Why?" The snappy dialogue continues: "Because I said so." Suddenly the situation has regressed from adult to adult to parent to child.

There is nothing that requires team leaders or employers to give team members reasons for doing what they ask . . . except common sense.

An intelligent adult needs an intelligent reason to be motivated.

The quick fix is compliance that comes from authority and intimidation. The fundamentals of motivation come from understanding team members and what is important to them.

Climate Control: Creating a Motivational Environment

There are two kinds of people: those who believe you can motivate others, and those who believe you can't. The first group believes that motivation can be external. The second group believes motivation is only internal. The first group is right.

From a practical standpoint, it doesn't really matter much whether motivation is internal or external.

Growing up I watched a lot of TV. One thing I learned from cops and robbers shows was that if you stroll into a bank and point a gun at the teller, chances are you'll get money. Now let's analyze this transaction. Have you motivated the teller or has the teller motivated himself? The answer is uncertain, but the outcome is clear: you got what you wanted.

This silly illustration makes an important point: what really happened in the bank was that you created an environment where it was easy for the teller to make the right decision (to give you the money). How does this apply to teamwork?

> *If you want people to be motivated, pay attention to the environment you create.*

It's unethical to manipulate people, but what's wrong with controlling the environment where your team does business? So what kind of environment is "motivational"? Going back to Bill Holekamp's definition, it is a place where people get the "stuff" they need to win. (For a wonderful explanation of the kind of environment employees want, read *A Great Place to Work* by Robert Levering.)

The best way to find out what your team members want from their

153

environment is to do a quality of life survey. Ask them questions such as:

- What do you like most about your work environment? Why?
- What do you like least? Why?
- If you could change only one thing about the work environment, what would it be?

This is not a scientific survey, but these questions will help you quickly ascertain what you need to do to develop a motivational environment.

You Get Back What You Put Out: Modeling Behavior

"Firings will continue until morale improves," reads a sign in the employee lunchroom.

The team leader sets the tone for the team. Negative leaders cannot expect positive followers. That's why the importance of leadership modeling behavior bears repeating.

> *You can't expect others to give back what you're not willing to put out.*

That applies to morale, attitude, and performance. Managers live in mirrored houses. If they don't like the reflection, they should change the source. Monitor your own example for insights into how team members are performing.

The Greatest Management Principle in the World

The foundation of motivation was beautifully explained in *The Greatest Management Principle in the World,* written by my good friend, Dr. Michael LeBoeuf. Knowing that readers don't remember concepts as well as they remember stories, he begins his book with this tale:

> *A weekend fisherman looked over the side of his boat*
> *and saw a snake with a frog in its mouth. Feeling sorry*
> *for the frog, he reached down, gently removed the frog*
> *from the snake's mouth and let the frog go free. But*
> *now he felt sorry for the hungry snake. Having no food,*
> *he took out a flask of bourbon and poured a few drops*
> *into the snake's mouth. The snake swam away happy,*
> *the frog was happy and the man was happy for having*
> *performed such good deeds. He thought all was well*
> *until a few minutes had passed and he heard*
> *something knock against the side of his boat and*
> *looked down. With stunned disbelief, the fisherman*
> *saw the snake was back—with two frogs!*

LeBoeuf goes on to explain the two important lessons of the fable. First, you get more of the behavior you reward. Secondly, in trying to do the right things, it is easy to fall into the trap of rewarding the wrong activities.

So what is the greatest management principle in the world?

> *The things that get rewarded get done.*

LeBoeuf understands the reality of the workplace. You don't get the behavior you demand, plead for, or hope for. You get the behavior you *reward.* Two fundamental rules of motivating team members:

1.   Reward the right behaviors.
2.   Use the right rewards.

Don't Ignore Good Performance

These concepts apply even if you are already getting the performance you want. Ever been puzzled by a team member who used to do good work, then mysteriously slid into mediocrity? Sometimes too much of a team leader's attention is directed toward team members who aren't performing, while team members who turn in a good performance are ignored. After all, why worry about them? Over time, some of those "ignored performers" start to wonder if their hard work and dedication are really worth it. They haven't been receiving feedback to validate that, so they begin to let performance slip a little. If performance slips enough, they will finally get the team leader's attention. Then the team leader wants to know, "What's wrong? You used to do such good work!"

The principle of extinction says behavior that is not rewarded will eventually cease. If there is no internal reward (some members will keep doing a good job, even if ignored, because their commitment and payoff are internal) or external recognition or reward, there is no motivation to perform. Don't ignore good performance. Apply the same principles of motivation if you want to keep strong performance at a consistent level.

Rewarding the Right Behaviors

To utilize the greatest management principle in the world, you must reward the right behaviors. What's "right" will depend on the type of work your team does and the performance you desire, but here are seven behaviors universally desirable in teambuilt organizations.

Reward Results, Not Activity. The first behavior to reward is *results,* or actual output. Unfortunately, what usually gets rewarded is *activity,* which is input.

Take the example of one mid-size printing company on the East Coast that is reasonably successful. The president prides himself on being a real slave driver. When he's in the office, people don't just work, they scramble. His office is purposely located by the door employees must use to leave the building, and he's let employees know that anybody seen leaving at 5 P.M. is suspect. In the boss's opinion, dedicated employees stay late (which usually means past 6 P.M.).

On the days when he's in the office, many employees do stay late, but not all are working. They socialize, use the company phones to call friends and relatives long distance, catch up on their reading, and generally kill time. But they're staying late—and that's what gets noticed and rewarded.

Things change when the president travels. His secretary, who has access to his travel schedule, alerts her friends when the president is going to be out of the office. Word circulates quickly, and on those days, some employees make it a point to come in late, take a long lunch, and leave early.

Such is the folly of focusing on activity instead of results. This manager looked favorably on the busiest people. Maybe it should follow that the people who work longest produce the most work, but that isn't always the case. What you can count on is that:

> *The most productive team members are those who get*
> *the most done, not those who work the longest hours.*

Despite this simple truth, lots of organizations continue to focus on activity rather than results. If you want results, reward results. Naïvely rewarding activity or long hours will get you more input, but it won't guarantee the output you desire. Wouldn't it be great to work in an organization where, if you produced the expected results by 3 P.M., you could take the rest of the day off? Or, if you chose, you could work later and get paid more for additional output?

Savvy team leaders focus on how productive the team is rather than how busy members appear. Team members are rewarded for their accomplishments instead of activity level.

Keep your team focused on results by talking results. On a regular basis—at least weekly—ask each team member to describe his or her greatest accomplishment for that time period. Focus on results and progress made toward results. Team members who are simply putting in time will have difficulty responding to such questions. ***Reward Team Members for Being Honest in Their Communication.*** Movie magnate Samuel Goldwyn is reputed to have said, "I don't want to be surrounded by 'yes men.' I want people to tell me what they think, even if it costs them their job." It's a funny line, but an unlikely scenario. In a team environment where people aren't rewarded for honesty, they may not lie—they just won't say much.

In teamwork, silence isn't golden, it's deadly.

Withheld opinions or partial ideas will destroy your efforts to team-build. Silent members will eventually turn your team into a work group in which one or two individuals are making decisions without input from those who have valuable information about how things should be done. Even worse, people who don't share their honest opinions often start to resent that they can't, and lose their commitment to the team.

Team members should be able to fight for what they feel is right. If their suggestions aren't implemented, it should be because the team decided to do something different on the basis of team merit— not because the suggestions weren't heard and considered.

Reward Team Members for Slaughtering Sacred Cows and Cutting Through Red Tape. Few things are more demotivating, time consuming, frustrating, and counterproductive to teamwork than bureaucracy and a highly regulated environment where there's a policy, procedure, or form for every decision or action.

In his book *Servant Leadership,* Robert Greenleaf describes one of the dangers of a highly regulated, bureaucratic environment: "When any action is regulated by law, the incentive for individual conscience to govern is diminished—unless the law coincides with almost universally held moral standards." An overreliance on bureaucracy—interally created rules, regulations, policies, procedures—diminishes the team's ability to think about what is being done. In the extreme, it results in the *sacred cow phenomenon.*

The sacred cow phenomenon works like this: the team, or more likely team management, makes rules and policies that make sense at the time of their creation. Team members are required to abide by these rules and policies—and they do. After a while, they stop challenging the rules and policies; the rules have become sacred. Then one day, the original reason for the rule changes. But nobody notices and they keep worshiping this sacred cow.

> *A sacred cow that has outlived its useful life should be made into hamburger.*

Reward team members who point out rules, policies, and procedures that no longer make sense. Give them an award for being an SOB—a Slayer of Bureaucracy. Encourage team members to challenge rules and procedures by asking at every team meeting: "What things do we ask you to do that either slow you down or make no sense to you?"

Reward Team Members for Exceeding Expected Performance Levels. The Philadelphia Zoo encourages employees to submit ideas about how to increase attendance. If attendance rises, all employees are rewarded for their ideas that contributed to the increase.

At the $1.5 billion Nucor Corp., teams are regularly rewarded for exceeding expectations. Ken Iverson, who heads Nucor, says, "Our success is based on groups working together: 25 to 35 people doing some task for which a standard is established. If they exceed that standard, they receive extra pay. At our steel mills, the average worker is making 140 percent of base pay because of overtime and performance incentives."

Develop a baseline of expected performance for the team and each member. Make sure that any performance that exceeds what is expected is recognized and rewarded.

Reward Team Members for Solving Problems, Rather than Just Spotting Them. Does your team suffer from external brain syndrome? Here's the scenario: they encounter a problem. Rather than do something, they unplug their brains and bring the problem to you. "What should we do?" they ask. "I'm busy right now," you reply. "Leave your brains on my desk and check back with me later." They do and spend the rest of the day wandering zombie-like around the department.

By mid-afternoon you've got a stack of brains on your desk. Many others have dropped off their brains so you could do their thinking for them. When you get a few extra minutes, you solve their problems, too. At the end of the day, just like a scene from *Night of the Living Dead,* the zombies show up to reclaim their brains. (They need them to drive home.) When they come in the next morning, they carry out your instructions.

The next time they face a problem, what do they do? They come to you, of course, because you have become their external brain. By inadvertently rewarding people for spotting problems, instead of solving them, you encourage them to become intellectually handicapped.

You can avoid external brain syndrome with your team by using a classic management technique. I know it works because one of my early managers tried it on me. I was going through the same "what should I do?" phase when my boss informed me one day, "Mark, I want you to feel free to come to me when there is a problem. However, anybody can spot a problem. Sometimes we call it moaning, groaning, and complaining. One of the reasons I hired you was to help me solve problems. From now on, whenever you come to me with a problem, I want you to come prepared with at least two possible solutions.

"Sometimes I'll let you try one of your solutions. Other times I'll discuss your ideas with you and see if we can't improve on them. But if you can't come up with any ideas, that probably means either the problem isn't important enough to deal with, or it's unsolvable. In that case, I don't need to hear about it."

Reward Team Members for Saving Money. Get rid of systems that reward team members for using up resources instead of using them wisely. Most managers review their budgets at the end of the fiscal year; if there's money left over, they know it creates an impression with management that they can operate with less money next year. So, to preserve future budgets, managers often get creative at using leftover funds, buying such stuff as new chairs that no one really needs.

One exception is a hospital in Flagstaff, Arizona, that's implemented a program called BYOB—Build Your Own Bonus. At the end of the year, if there is any money left in a department's budget, the employees in that department get 10 percent to split among themselves. Employees treat hospital money like it's their own (and in a way, it is).

Phillips Petroleum is another employer that awards employees up to 10 percent of any cost savings that employees come up with. In 1987, 81 percent of Phillips's employees suggested ideas that saved the company $16.5 million. That's the power of rewarding employees for saving money.

Reward Exceptional Service—to Customers or Other Team Members. Customer service is a noble concept but it doesn't go far enough. Not all team members have contact with traditional customers in the marketplace—but all employees serve someone in their work. Teams need to commit to "the service ethic": *Since everybody serves somebody, serve whoever that is exceptionally well.* Customer service is created inside out. Which means that the better you serve team members and other teams in your organization, the better they'll be able to serve their customers. To achieve legendary customer service, make it a point to reward anyone on the team for any exceptional act of service.

The Problem with Tree Repairman

One bright summer day I was strolling across the patio at the Hilton in Bakersfield, California. Two repairmen were suspended from a tree. As I walked by, one looked at his watch and said to the other, "We better hurry if we're going to get any more trees done today." And his partner said, "What's the big hurry? It doesn't matter how much we get done. The boss will still make his million dollars and we won't get paid a nickel more."

That repairman's philosophy will plague any organization that doesn't provide effective performance incentives.

Organizations that fail to link reward to performance usually fail to get performance worth rewarding.

Using the Right Rewards

By my definition, motivation = money + meaning. Neither money nor meaning alone will elicit optimal performance from team members. Just as some employers overemphasize money, others rely too much on employees' search for satisfaction and significance. Money can be an effective motivator when used as both a reward and a scorecard. With pay linked to performance, team members get turned on by both economic incentive and the challenge of doing better.

What Are You Paying Your Team Members For?

In Little Rock, Arkansas, a 27-year-old manufacturing employee told me he was one of the youngest people in his company to become assistant foreman. Before the promotion, his boss had promised him a significant increase in salary if he earned the position. Furthermore, if he met certain performance objectives as assistant foreman, he would qualify for another increase in six months. He had done both, and received the promised pay increases.

But when his boss's boss found out how much the relatively young man was being paid, he hit the ceiling, demanding to know, "How can you justify paying a 27-year-old this much money?"

The wise manager replied, "I'm not paying him for his age, I'm paying him for his performance."

That makes more sense than paying employees on the basis of age, education, or tenure—all of which weigh heavily in traditional compensation systems. (Education could justify increased pay *if* the education adds value to an employee's performance.)

Performance-based compensation equals roughly 27 percent of a Japanese employee's total pay. But in the U.S., performance-based compensation is only $9/10$ of 1 percent!

> *To make teamwork work, find ways to link pay to performance.*

Profit sharing and gain sharing are the two most common means of accomplishing this in for-profit organizations. Profit sharing gives some percentage of profits to employees. While this is a worthwhile system, it rewards individuals on the basis of organizational performance.

Gain sharing gives a percentage of gains (increased productivity or decreased costs) to the individual or team responsible for the gains. If your team is able to increase output, some predetermined percentage of that monetary gain is given to the team. Gain sharing can also be structured on an individual basis.

THE QUESTION MOST TEAM MEMBERS HAVE NEVER BEEN ASKED

While doing some informal research on motivation in the mid-'80s, I was surprised to find that less than 10 percent of the 250 middle managers I talked to had ever been asked one basic but very important question. Without knowing the answer, you'll never be able to effectively motivate team members—that's why I call this the million-dollar question of motivation:

What motivates you?

Unfortunately, we all walk around with a cookie-cutter mentality. We figure, "Hey, people are people, and if something hits my hot button, it must hit yours too." But the thinking leader knows this is a fatal assumption. Alex McEachern once said, "No matter how much you like vegetables yourself, never try to feed a cat a carrot."

You motivate different people differently.

Recall the memorable line from the prayer of St. Francis, "Lord, grant that I may not seek so much to be understood as to understand." The only way you can get in touch with how to motivate an individual is by observing and asking. To get you started, here are seven questions you can ask team members to find out what hits their hot buttons and motivates them.

What Do You Like Most About Your Job? If you know what a team member likes to do, you can reward him by giving him more of that to do for a day or a week, or, if it makes sense, restructure his responsibilities so he does that on a regular basis.

What Do You Like Least About Your Job? After question one, this comes as no surprise. One way to reward people is to temporarily relieve them of responsibilities they find burdensome.

What Would You Like to Do in the Future? Get in touch with the career aspirations and personal goals of the people you're trying to motivate. Let them know that if they perform, you're going to help them achieve those personal goals.

What Would You Most Like to Learn and What Training or Education Would That Require? You'll find that most team members have an agenda of job-related skills they'd like to develop, or an area of expertise they'd like to learn. Rewarding performance with educational opportunities provides a double benefit.

When Do You Feel You Do Your Best Work? Unless a team member is highly interdependent with other members, why not give him the flexibility of determining when he starts and stops work each day? Leading-edge companies realize that *when* employees do their work is less important than *how well* they do it. Currently, approximately 35 percent of U.S. companies utilize some form of flexible working hours for some or all of their employees.

Who Do You Work with Best? This isn't the same as asking team members who they enjoy working with most. This question identifies who team members feel they interact with best to create results. It goes beyond enjoyment to the more practical issue of productivity. Often, however, those people we work with best turn out to be those we also enjoy most.

What Gives You the Most Pride in Your Work? This is slightly different from asking what someone most likes to do. This question identifies a team member's greatest source of pride, which may come from a difficult challenge he or she has overcome, a sense of belonging, or any number of factors. Recognizing an individual's source of pride is a powerful motivator.

Unlike the cookie-cutter approach to motivation that is traditionally used, these questions help team leaders identify the diversity of values, wants, and desires within a team, and provide the information necessary to tailor motivation to individual team members.

COSTS LITTLE, PAYS MUCH

Linking pay to performance may not be feasible, especially if your team operates in the public sector or a nonprofit environment. Fortunately, there are a number of nonmonetary rewards you can utilize. The only limitation is your imagination. Here are a few ideas to stimulate your thinking.

Submit an Article to the Company Newsletter. Spotlight team members as well as the whole team. Jot down a few sentences about an unusual accomplishment a team member has made.

At Avon Products Inc., teamwork regularly makes headlines in the company's worldwide newsletter, *Outlook.* One such example is a March 1991 story billed "Atlanta rallies to No. 1" that describes how teamwork revived sagging spirits, and improved service and sales at one of the company's U.S. distribution facilities. Appearing in the January 1992 issue, under the headline "Team approach earns Avon-U.K. a banner year," is another account of how teamwork is helping the company dominate its market and produce double-digit profits. And currently scheduled for publication: a story on how teams of employees at Avon-Australia pulled off a top-to-bottom revitalization that reversed a six-year sales slump—despite the fact that Australia is suffering its worst recession since World War II.

Outlook editor Alan Marks says he welcomes news tips from employees: "I'm always looking for stories that highlight teamwork. Such stories help make all employees more aware that our company's success is the result of people working together, not just a few talented individuals. Invariably, behind every successful strategy is a team of employees who believed in a common goal."

Give 'Em a Break. CareerTrack, a leading seminar training company in Boulder, Colorado, has a good idea for rewarding trainers: a coupon that says "Take A Break On Us!" The back of the coupon says, "At CareerTrack, we think you're terrific! And to show you our appreciation, take a break—on us. This coupon is good for $15 toward any activity of your choice. To redeem, simply attach a receipt to this coupon and send it to Accounts Payable . . ." It goes on to list some suggestions: Call home, or an old friend . . . Order room service (Häagen-Dazs, perhaps) . . . Go to a movie and eat lots of popcorn . . . Get a pizza with all the extras.

Involve Higher-ups. Ask the CEO of your organization to write a personal note of appreciation to a team member. Sometimes middle managers are frustrated because upper management doesn't practice teambuilding techniques. Here's a way to draw upper management in without their even knowing it.

Tell the CEO, plant manager, or agency director—whoever you are trying to involve—about something outstanding a team member has done. Ask the person to write a brief note of appreciation. Better yet, if you've explained the accomplishment in a memo, the person can simply add a personal note on the memo. Then give the memo to the team member, who will see that you shared news of the accomplishment and that upper management noticed.

Be sure to give your organizational leader feedback on how much the note meant to the team member (assuming, of course, that it did). The idea is to subtly condition higher-ups to make more of these little gestures, such as note writing—without being asked.

Set Up a Peer Recognition Program. Some years ago I presented a program for the City of Mansfield Public School. I talked about the importance of recognition and confirmation that a team member's efforts were valued. Some of the teachers decided that if they waited for their "customers" (the students) to give them recognition and confirmation, they would probably retire before it happened.

With the help of school leadership, a program called "Praise A Peer" was instituted. They printed up note cards with "Praise A Peer" on the front; the inside was blank. Everyone got a bunch of cards with instructions that whenever you caught a colleague doing something worthwhile, you were to write a brief note of appreciation and leave it in his or her mailbox. The goal was to give away all your cards by the end of the year. This is an excellent example of a peer recognition program.

Vary the Team Members' Responsibilities. Very often, variety motivates people. Just break their routines by giving them less of the work they don't like or more of the work they do. Or maybe even change their work or level of responsibility.

If you have team members who are almost burned out, reward them by saying, "You know, for the next couple of weeks, I'm going to assign you some relatively light duty, so you'll have a chance to rejuvenate and recharge your batteries."

Offer Time Rewards. These might include flex time, time off, allowing a team member to come in an hour later than normal or leave an hour early, and extending their lunch break.

Let Team Members Come Up with Their Own Titles. Since you have an organizational mission statement, and a team mission, why not let team members have some fun by creating their own titles? John Scully, CEO at Apple, says if he were to pick his own title, it would be "Chief Listening Officer." Some unusual titles at Apple include Hardware Wizard and Software Evangelist. Allowing a team member to choose their title based on what they're most proud of creates a kind of micro-mission statement.

My friend Antonia Boyle at Cassette Production Unlimited has this title on her business card: Empress of Audio. She's had that title for some time, bringing it with her from her last job at a different organization.

Here's a variation. Take the titles they already have, and when team members have performed at high levels, add the word "extraordinaire" as a sign of special accomplishment.

Put Team Members in the Public Spotlight. Did you ever stop to think about the fact that every newspaper in America is looking for copy fillers, especially in the business section? Promotions make good news items. Trade publications look for little articles about who's doing what in the industry. Yet few managers take the time to send a memo or press release to those magazines and newspapers. Getting people public recognition is motivational.

Use Training as a Reward. Let the team members each pick a seminar of their choice or buy a book or tapes series they're interested in. Look at training as a double win—nonmonetary recognition and reward.

Track Accomplishments

One study found that managers miss up to 83 percent of the good things their employees do. If this is only half true, it's a problem.

If you are a team leader, ask members to document their significant contributions to the team each quarter. If you have performance evaluations once or twice a year, it's important that team members track their own contributions and how they're adding value. Ask them to periodically review their accomplishments by writing a one-paragraph summary of each accomplishment and why they think it is important. When you conduct their performance evaluations, ask them to pick their six or eight most important accomplishments. Since they've already written paragraphs for these, they can easily combine the paragraphs into a mini-report.

11

STEP 6: CELEBRATE

EVALUATING AND CELEBRATING TEAM ACCOMPLISHMENT

The sixth and, in my opinion, *most overlooked* step in teambuilding is evaluation and celebration. Team leadership needs to frequently ask the team, "Are we making progress or regress?"

How do teambuilt organizations do this? Success can be evaluated against the standards of the holographic team:

- moving closer to the vision
- fulfilling the mission
- achieving the goals
- upholding values
- meeting expectations

It follows then that

> *Celebration acknowledges both accomplishment and effort.*

21 QUESTIONS FOR EVALUATING WHETHER YOUR TEAMWORK WORKS

Regardless of where your organization is in its efforts to build team-work, the most important consideration isn't *how good are you at teambuilding?*, but *how good could you be?*

To assist you in your evaluation, I have developed 21 questions you need to answer to make teamwork work. As you answer "yes" or "no," jot down some notes about *why* you answered that way, and *what you can do to improve.*

1. *Are you involving your team members in hiring decisions?* You live with a bad hiring decision, on average, for 18 months. Yet, what management considers a good hiring decision and what team members consider a good hiring decision may be dramatically different. Let team members meet potential new hires before an offer is made. Factor their feedback into the decision.

2. *Do you know who your team slayers are and have you taken steps to deal with the problem?* Have you identified team slayers—those individuals whose behavior detracts from team performance—and have you spent time with them diagnosing the reasons why and what to do about them?

3. *Do team members understand the team's vision, mission, goals, values, and expectations?* These are the blueprint for the team's success, so members must have a crystal-clear understanding of these important components.

4. *Are team members committed to the team's success?* This is a situation where simply asking isn't enough—look for outward manifestations of commitment. More likely, it will be easier to spot a lack of commitment. Excessive questioning of why people are being asked to do what they do is one

171

sign. Complaining, lack of performance, low morale—all suggest that commitment to vision, mission, values, goals, and expectations may be lacking.

5. *Have team members been trained in teamwork skills?* Is your teambuilding curriculum in place? Training should be ongoing, and whenever possible, team members should attend sessions as a group.

6. *Have team leaders been trained for their roles?* There are some natural born leaders, but not enough for most organizations. Leadership skills must be developed. In addition to basic team skills, team leaders need special training in areas such as group facilitation and mediation.

7. *Have you started building relationships with future team members?* Someday you're going to lose team members— they'll quit, move away, or go to another team within the organization. When you receive notice they're leaving, you'll need to have potential replacements identified and, if possible, already thinking about joining the team. Relationship building with potential team members needs to be done well in advance.

8. *Are you holding regular team meetings that participants find worthwhile?* Regularly ask team members to assess the effectiveness of team meetings. If they feel the meetings are wasting their time, you're either meeting too frequently or preparing inadequately. If team members don't feel informed, you may not be meeting enough.

9. *Do team meetings include both information and motivation?* You've got to have both. I like to use the analogy of cherry-flavored cough syrup. When you buy cherry-flavored cough syrup, your primary motivation is medicinal—you want to suppress the cough. Because if you really just wanted cherry flavor, you'd buy soda pop. So why

flavor the cough syrup? To help the medicine go down more easily. Likewise, you should make meetings interesting, entertaining, and motivational to help the information go down more easily. Team members need both "how-to" and "want-to."

10. *Is interpersonal communication effective?* Team communication should provide information members can use: news rather than gossip, and feedback rather than criticism. Do team members share useful information with each other in an open, honest environment?

11. *Do team members feel well informed about news of the larger organization?* It's important that teams don't operate in a vacuum. They should understand how they fit into the big picture and how they impact the organization's performance. Top managers and others outside the team should be utilized as resources.

12. *What efforts has your team or entire organization made to create interdepartmental teamwork?* Even harder than getting people on the same team to work together is getting people on different teams to work together. Have you made some active attempts to teambuild with other departments in your organization?

13. *Is your team facing some of the same problems today that they were 60 days ago, and if so, why?* Ignoring significant problems won't help. After two months, problems that remain unsolved are either insignificant or overdue for attention. Deal with problems before they become a source of perpetual frustration for team members.

14. *What feedback has your team given to management and how has management responded?* At one large organization on the East Coast, a team leader told me one of his greatest frustrations was that his boss was a "yes man"

who didn't represent the needs of their team to management. Does your team or team leader communicate ideas and needs to management? If so, has management responded appropriately and convinced team members that their opinions are valued?

15. *Have you, as team leader, taken time to understand the values, likes, dislikes, and needs of every team member?* Because different people are motivated differently, if you haven't done your homework in understanding what motivates different members, you aren't as far along in teambuilding as you could be.

16. *Does the team deal openly and effectively with conflict?* Have team members learned to use all available approaches to conflict resolution and agreed on a system that allows the team to deal with the problems that inevitably arise? Pursuing the team vision should be the primary agenda, even in difficult times.

17. *Are all team members open to feedback?* Or is feedback accepted only from the team leader? When a team member has an idea that will help another member improve performance, is it offered?

18. *Can you point to specific innovations that your team has made in the past quarter?* Are you creating new ideas or simply doing things the same way you always did and maintaining the status quo? Make sure to reward any attempts at innovation, even when the outcome isn't successful. Challenge team members to try new things.

19. *Are you operating with a team calendar year?* Teams must be accountable for producing results in time. Have you identified top team goals for the current calendar year and do members know what those goals are? Use action planning at every team session to translate ideas into results.

20. *Do team members see the link between individual success and team success?* Do you reward and recognize people, not just for what they personally accomplish, but for how they contribute to helping the team accomplish its goals? Team members must experience this critical linkage if teamwork is going to work.

21. *What celebrations, formal and informal, have you undertaken to demonstrate appreciation and create camaraderie?* Evaluate results periodically. Regularly and creatively celebrate the team's efforts and victories. If you're lucky, you'll receive accolades from others, but you can't really control that. Ultimately, it is your responsibility to celebrate your team's success.

These questions recap some of the most important issues covered previously, but you may want to develop additional assessment questions of your own; ask team members what questions they think should be used to evaluate team performance. Remember, a team's opinions count as much as the leader's, so actively involve everyone in evaluating current success and planning future improvements. The team meeting is a good time and place to do such periodic evaluations.

WHY CELEBRATE?

If most organizations don't evaluate enough, they celebrate even less. After all, evaluation is at least a concept taught in business school. Celebration is a social concept; the word doesn't even sound businesslike. We're talking about *work* here, so why celebrate? Celebration provides a number of benefits to teams that practice it.

Celebration Communicates That Everyone's Contributions Are Appreciated. Celebration is one important way an organization says "thank you" for the good things members do individually and collectively.

Several years ago, the three founders of a California company got up in the wee hours of the morning to cook a pancake breakfast for their 300-plus employees. Imagine the unusual scene employees were treated to: the chairman of the board pouring orange juice, the CEO flipping pancakes, and the CFO serving up scrambled eggs. Has upper management at your organization ever cooked a meal for you?

When the business media learned about the event, someone from the press asked the three busy executives why they didn't have the function catered. After all, considering the value of their time, doing the cooking themselves wasn't cost-effective. Demonstrating insight and wisdom, these executives captured the spirit of celebration by responding that it was critically important for every employee in their organization to know that the founders personally appreciated their hard work and dedication. And what better way to show that (and have some fun in the process) than by cooking breakfast for everyone?

Celebration Helps Create and Maintain Camaraderie. Celebration is both a cause and an effect of camaraderie. Sometimes celebration occurs because of the camaraderie that exists between team members; other times, celebration helps create camaraderie. Invariably, the two work together.

Japanese giant Sony Corp. regards social interaction among employees as so important that it built a nightclub on company headquarters' property. Called the Sony Club, it is a safe and convenient place for employees to celebrate, get to know each other better, and share ideas. (Another benefit: Sony doesn't have to worry about employees drinking too much and divulging secrets that could be overheard by competitors.)

Celebrating Helps Relieve Stress. Teambuilt organizations can be intense places to work. It is refreshing to occasionally have times when it is OK to "kick back and let your hair down." (Warning: celebrating too much can also create stress.)

Celebration Is Fun. Infusing the workplace with fun empowers team members and delights the customers they serve. Herb Kelleher is the unorthodox leader of Southwest Airlines, a $1.2 billion company with 9,500 employees known for their loyalty and team spirit. Kelleher regularly mingles with front-line employees and talks with passengers while serving as a flight attendant. Known for his comic antics, he once showed up at a hangar on Halloween night dressed in drag as Corporal Klinger from "M*A*S*H" to thank mechanics for working overtime.

Tips for Celebrating

You might think celebrating comes naturally to groups of people, but there's little evidence to support that. Other than sponsoring the sometimes anticipated—but often dreaded—Christmas party, the typical organization doesn't seem to celebrate much and they certainly don't celebrate creatively. Here are a few celebration pointers.

Celebrate Regularly. At least once a quarter, schedule some type of formal celebration that team members will look forward to. One Denver-based software company celebrates more frequently by holding "First Friday Parties." The first Friday of each month, they quit work at 3:30 P.M. and meet at a local restaurant or club for drinks and hors d'oeuvres.

Be Creative in How You Celebrate. Sales organizations hold some pretty elaborate celebrations. One example is a high-tech company that rented the local football stadium to celebrate the accomplishments of its salespeople. Friends and relatives filled the stands. Guests were given confetti, and a marching band was on hand to provide upbeat music. As the top sellers were introduced over loudspeakers, they ran onto the field while the band played, and

177

enthusiastic friends and relatives greeted them with confetti. Now all that may seem a little corny, but it had to have been great fun.

The only drawback of elaborate celebrations is that they're usually expensive. Stadiums and marching bands aren't cheap. Sometimes, celebrations should be elaborate; other times, something much more low-key is effective, as my third tip shows.

Try the "Dollars to Donuts" Approach. Celebrations don't have to be big or extravagant to be worthwhile. I was visiting a friend in Fort Worth, Texas, who worked for a prestigious law firm located downtown in posh, high-rise offices. The morning of my visit, I was given a tour of the offices and introduced to some of the lawyers and staff, all of whom were impeccably dressed in conservative business attire. This was a dignified group.

About 9:30 A.M., a secretary showed up with a couple of boxes of donuts. The only way I can describe the scene that ensued is to compare it to sharks in a feeding frenzy: the energy level in the office rose instantly and formerly sedate people were grabbing for their favorite donuts. I've never seen so much powdered sugar on expensive suits.

If donuts can get a group of lawyers that excited, think about how often your team gets donuts in the morning. Now I'm not suggesting that you make the consumption of junk food a basis for your team's celebrations—but you may want to think about some small, inexpensive gestures that will make great brief, informal celebrations.

Why Not "Edubrate"? In the fall of 1990, David Murphy, president of the Betty Crocker Products division of General Mills, invited all 200 local employees to the Minneapolis Metrodome for a special event in their honor. At the event, called "Beyond the Limits," employees were asked to forget their fears and try three new experiences. Activities included rappelling a 100-foot fake mountain, windsurfing, pitching baseballs to a Twin, throwing footballs to a Viking, and even performing stand-up comedy. Although the aim was to boost employee morale, creativity, and confidence, the event, as described later in *Fortune* magazine, must have included many fun moments for all involved.

Think about combining education with celebration, and you've got an *edubration.*

Encourage Informal Celebration Among Team Members. It would be a sign of great team health if once a week every member had breakfast with another member, just to get to know one other better and share ideas. Celebrations can be spontaneous and don't always need to involve the whole team. If three or four members worked together on a special project, let them celebrate together when it's completed.

Make Celebration Planning a Team Activity. Ask team members how they would like to celebrate. Find out what's important to them. Brainstorm ideas for a creative celebration session. An example would be donating several hours to a local charitable organization and having a cookout afterward. Allocate some part of your budget for quarterly team celebrations and involve the team in deciding how to spend the money.

If You Don't, Nobody Else Will

In 1986 a team leader from a Midwestern telephone company who was attending one of my teambuilding seminars shared this experience about the importance of celebrating team success.

Several months earlier, her team of customer service reps had set a company record: 100 percent customer satisfaction for an entire month. Whenever a customer called with a complaint, her team had been able to resolve the problem to the customer's complete satisfaction. This had never been done before. Company management was delighted and rewarded the team with a very nice celebration.

Everyone on this team, which happened to be composed of

women, received flowers. Then the company treated them and their spouses to a terrific evening at a local dinner theater. The team was very impressed with how they were treated.

But the story doesn't end there. The team leader told me that a week later, she took the team out for pizza and beer—her treat.

Given the lavish celebration the team had just received, I asked, wasn't the beer and pizza a case of overkill? Her answer revealed an important lesson I've observed many times since.

She said, "The reason for the celebration was our record-setting performance for one month. Management couldn't help but notice that. Next time we achieve the same performance level, they'll say 'Keep up the good work.' The third time we do something note-worthy, they will have expected it. Even if we keep our performance level high, we're bound to have an off-month someday. And when we do, management will probably ask 'What's wrong with your team?' *The better we perform, the less our good performance will be noticed. That's why it is our responsibility to always celebrate our own success.* If we don't, we can't always count on somebody else to do it for us."

You may have already experienced this with your own team. It is a paradox of sorts, but in some organizations:

> *The longer your team performs well, the less team performance will be celebrated.*

That's because expectations of the team will rise as team perform-ance rises. Whether your employer celebrates your success is not a circumstance within your control. But you can celebrate your own team success. If you don't, nobody else will.

12

TAKING THE TEAM THROUGH TOUGH TIMES

In the deep South just prior to the Civil War there lived a poor sharecropper who took joy from the two most important things in his life: his strong, healthy teenage son and his beautiful brown workhorse. One day the horse got loose and disappeared into the woods. The farmer fell into a depression.

Several days later, the horse came back, followed by a wild gray horse. The man was overjoyed. He quickly captured both horses and marveled over his luck.

The son was anxious to break the wild horse. But the first time he rode it, he was thrown, badly breaking both legs in the process. The farmer's joy at his newfound luck turned to grief.

The next week a Confederate general made a sweep of the countryside to recruit young men to join the war against the North. Coming to the farmer's residence, he demanded to see the son. But when the general saw the young man's condition, he knew he was unfit to be a soldier and left him behind. Once again, the farmer rejoiced.

And the farmer's life continued to be a cycle of good fortune and tragedy, disappointment and joy.

AND SO IT GOES

Like life, business comes in cycles. At the writing of this book, the U.S. economy continues to languish in a recession. Everyone expects a recovery—nobody knows when. Challenging times are nothing new. It's just that our memories are short. When things are good, it is easy to forget when they were bad. When things are bad, it is difficult to remember that they were ever good.

No matter how much success your team currently enjoys, you will encounter problems in the future, just as you did in the past. Some will be short-term, a brief blip on the monitor. Others could be severe and result in a serious setback. Even optimists know that difficulties are inevitable.

It is fascinating that even during difficult times, some organizations prosper. Even more unusual is when an organization is experiencing difficulty, but a division, region, or group within it is doing better than ever. That group or team becomes a bright spot in the dismal picture of the overall organization.

Some teams die when times are tough, others survive. A few find ways to thrive.

In studying organizations and teams dealing with difficulty, I've observed some common coping strategies, attitudes, and behaviors. Here are the most practical and common, which I've grouped into a list of *thrival tactics* that can be used to survive and even prosper in difficult times.

Thrival Tactic #1: Anticipate Difficulty

Expect problems and challenges. Alan Loy McGinnis, therapist and best-selling author, says, "Optimists are seldom surprised by problems. Instead of being surprised, they simply start looking for solutions." To be solution-oriented means combining acceptance with anticipation. As a team, accept that there will be difficulties and anticipate how you might respond.

To avoid being blindsided, ask "what if" questions:

- What if we lose some of our team members to another team?
- What if there are cutbacks in resources?
- What if the deadline we have been given is moved ahead two weeks?
- What if the product we make is discontinued?
- What if we lose our biggest customer?

Be careful not to raise unnecessary concerns, but be realistic about what might occur. Being able to talk about a problem, real or potential, aids one's ability to deal with it.

Thrival Tactic #2: Admit Difficulties, but Don't Belabor Them

When difficulties do occur, the first step in dealing with them is acknowledging they exist. Teams and team leaders can spend much time in unhealthy denial (after all, entire industries do this). The potential danger in acknowledging difficulties is that a team begins to belabor them. A victim-mentality develops: "We don't deserve this. It isn't fair. How can we be expected to deal with this?"

It is important to acknowledge negative emotions such as frustration and worry. Denying honest emotions is no more helpful than denying real problems. But dwelling on either usually only increases negativity. The key is to move quickly from negative emotion to positive action. The important question to ask is, "What can we do to solve, eliminate, or minimize the problem?"

Thrival Tactic #3: Equip Team Members for Handling Difficulties

A few team members may be well-prepared to cope with difficulty, because of temperament, past experience, or education. But what about the others?

Organizations tend to suffer from what I call *the training paradox.* It works like this: "When times are good, we feel we don't need to train our people. When times are bad, we feel we can't afford to train them." But the reality is that training, to be effective, must occur during good times and bad.

In Copenhagen, Denmark, an audience member approached me during the break. "I like to go to seminars," this young employee told me. "I read a lot of books, use audio cassettes and videos, and attend programs like these. The problem is my boss. He's an old-style manager, and he feels because these seminars and tapes don't add anything to the bottom line, they're a waste of time. He says any time not spent doing my primary job is unproductive time."

I shared with this young man a familiar story that merits repeating. Two lumberjacks in the northwestern United States were arguing one evening over who was the better lumberjack. They decided the only way to resolve the dispute was to have a wood-chopping competition. They would get up at sunrise the next day and start chopping. When the sun set, whoever had chopped the most wood would be the winner.

The next morning, they began the contest. The first lumberjack was amazing: he worked straight through the day without stopping to rest or eat. The second lumberjack did stop occasionally, which made the first lumberjack confident of victory.

At the end of the day, the first lumberjack was dismayed to discover the second had actually chopped more wood. He challenged him: "I worked longer and harder than you. You stopped to rest and still you've chopped more wood. How can this be?" The winning lumberjack replied, "I did stop several times during the day, but it wasn't to rest. I stopped to sharpen my axe."

The lesson in this story: The less time and money a team has for training, the more important training becomes. During difficult times team members are often asked to work longer and harder. But if they aren't given training resources—the time to sharpen their axes— they end up like losing lumberjacks, puzzled and disappointed at their lack of results.

Thrival Tactic #4: Don't Ask for Sacrifices That Aren't Shared

During difficult times such as a recession, employers often ask employees to accept pay and benefit freezes, or even cutbacks. Employees usually make such sacrifices because they don't have a choice.

But do managers and leaders share in these sacrifices? Are their salaries and benefits frozen or cut proportionately? And when there is an upturn in the economy or the company's business, does management remember to reward those who sacrificed by sharing new or regained profits with them?

Employees are sick of one-sided sacrifice. Teambuilt organizations understand that what takes team members through difficult times is the knowledge of shared sacrifice and the hope of shared gain.

Thrival Tactic #5: Beware of Non-Team Agendas

An excellent book on teamwork was written by Carl Larson and Frank LaFasto. It's called *Teamwork: What Must Go Right, What*

Can Go Wrong. The authors found that ". . . in the descriptions of ineffectively functioning teams the factor that occurred far more frequently than any other was very simple: The team had raised— or had allowed to become raised—some other issue or focus above the team's performance objective. Something was being attended to that had assumed, at least at that time, a higher priority than the team's goal."

I call these conflicting issues "non-team agendas." When a personal or non-team agenda starts to drive part, or all, of the team's efforts, there is serious trouble. Team leaders and members need to be vigilant against these non-team agendas. When they arise, they need to be addressed. The team's perspective can be restored and its energies redirected by evaluating any decision or issue on the basis of team merit.

In 1969, Hanover Insurance was nearly bankrupt. Today, their 19 percent compound rate of return ranks them 16th out of 68 companies in the insurance industry— even though Hanover handles one-tenth of the volume of industry giants like Aetna. By working hard to create a corporate philosophy that is more in line with human nature, Hanover has been able to achieve an organizational cohesiveness that makes teamwork work.

One of Hanover's guiding principles is *merit.* Merit means making decisions based on the best interests of the organization. Similarly, if a team's agenda is congruent with the organization's agenda, then team merit means making decisions based on what's best for the team, or in other words, keeping the team's agenda first.

Merit comes into play when the team must make a decision that is not popular with every member. Some may dislike or even disagree with the decision. But the decision is valid if it represents the best interests of the team and there is agreement that team members will support it for that reason. Team merit reminds team members that although personal and other issues may be relevant, the good of the team cannot be sacrificed for those non-team agendas.

Thrival Tactic #6: Watch Out for Situational Team Slayers

Problematic team players can become team slayers. There are also situations that can slay teamwork. Here are eight situational team slayers and what to do about them.

The First Is Inability to Deal with Change. In their 1982 bestseller, *In Search of Excellence,* Tom Peters and Bob Waterman talked about 43 of the most excellent companies in America. Within 24 months, 14 of those companies—fully 35 percent—were in financial trouble. Critics said Peters and Waterman had picked the wrong companies. But *BusinessWeek* said the reason those 14 companies were in trouble was their failure to react and respond to change.

Clearly, excellence is not a destination, but a journey. Losing one's way occurs when the forces of change are ignored. The solution to the first situational team slayer: learn to deal with change, to reassess the team environment and strategies, and to respond appropriately.

The Second Situational Team Slayer Is Prejudice Caused by Differences. The Japanese base the success of their teams on conformity and uniformity. In Japan they say, "The nail that sticks out gets pounded in." In the United States, teams gain strength from diversity and cooperation, the fact that people with different background, skills, and abilities can work together despite their differences. But for that to happen a team must be able to accept differences without placing negative judgments on them. Even better, as a team I worked with at AT&T says, "We've really learned to value individual differences, not just accept them."

The Third Situational Team Slayer Is the Pendulum Effect. Aristotle advanced the concept of the golden mean, which states that a virtue is midway between two excesses. For instance, one of the keys to teamwork is interdependence. The two excesses are over-dependence—people who won't do anything without depending on others for help—and independence—people who survive on the basis of their ability alone.

The pendulum effect is the tendency to go too far and miss the golden mean. Any suggestion in this book will, if taken to an extreme, negate teambuilding efforts. For example, in an effort to encourage team member involvement, leaders can ask for too much input and get employees bogged down in decision making. In attempting to provide team direction, a well-meaning team leader can assume too much control. The pendulum effect can take you too far in either direction and cause you to miss the intended result, or golden mean.

The Fourth Situational Team Slayer: Tradition as Anchor. A friend who works for a very staid bureaucracy says, "I work in an organization anchored in tradition and not hampered by progress." While a team can benefit from a long history of tradition, sometimes the things that brought the team to where it is may not be able to continue taking the team where it needs to go. Teambuilt organizations know

Tradition should serve as a foundation, not as an anchor.

One of the most difficult things a team must decide is what parts of tradition are viable in a current situation and represent irrevocable values to which the team is committed.

The Fifth Situational Team Slayer Is Unrealistic Expectations. Team leaders need to monitor and balance three sets of expectations: what management expects, what team members expect, and what the leader expects of team members. An informed team leader who is familiar with resources and restraints must intuitively make decisions about when an expectation is realistic. If management's expectations are unrealistic, the team leader must persuasively negotiate for different expectations or more resources. If a team member's expectations are unrealistic, the team leader needs to diplomatically bring that person back to reality to avoid future disappointment. And if the team leader's expectations aren't met, he or she needs to objectively assess if the team fell short—or the expectation was set too high. Realistic expectations determine success and happiness in advance. Unrealistic expectations lock in failure and disappointment.

Situational Team Slayer Six Is the Need to Control People. In any work environment, team or nonteam, successful managers know it is their job to control results, not people. Team members can also fall into the trap of trying to control others to get the results they desire—they need to understand that the ultimate and only real control is self-control. Successful people learn to overcome their inability to control others by controlling their own interactions and responses. If a team member is unhappy with another's behavior, look at the result and see if the end justifies the means. If the means are ethical and fair to others, then the results achieved may well be more important than how they are achieved. We all want to control others, but that need, unchecked, can kill teamwork.

Slayer Seven Is the Unwillingness to Fail. William Lear, inventor of the jet engine, intentionally created things he knew would fail. One example was his steam car. Why would an inventor intentionally pursue an idea he knew was doomed? Lear believed that *the price of innovation was the willingness to purposely fail.*

As a skier, I know that falling is seldom fun, but it is a sign of learning. Failure that is not injurious is constructive. The team that isn't making mistakes isn't trying anything different, and even worse, they're not learning anything new.

The Eighth Situational Team Slayer Is Certainty of the Future. If you're certain of what the future looks like, you get blindsided by the changes in store. Theologians call it the "omnipotence factor," the all-knowing attitude which says that since we know what the future looks like, the plans we make today will never have to change. Beware of an unshakable certainty of the future.

These thrival tactics are useful ideas—not ironclad guarantees that aim to improve your team's ability to survive difficult times. There will be some problems that defy solution and some difficulties that appear insurmountable. What can your team do when you've tried everything and nothing seems to work?

Teams are often asked to do "more with less" or deal with problems they neither created nor deserve. The ability to accept with grace the injustices of an imperfect world distinguishes a high performance team. I'm not suggesting a Pollyanna attitude that says "Everything will be all right if we just believe." What's needed is a realistic appraisal of the situation and an effort to take responsibility for maximizing results despite the physical limitations. With this in mind, I've written the "Team Creed for Dealing with Challenges and Difficulties." Feel free to copy it and use it in your own teambuilding efforts.

TEAM CREED FOR DEALING WITH CHALLENGES AND DIFFICULTIES

We believe difficulties are inevitable. We commit to anticipate and avoid difficulties to the degree that we can. When difficult times occur, we will remember that how we respond as a team is more important than why the difficulties occurred.

We recognize that any organization conducts its business within a framework prescribed by the marketplace and influenced by the organization's leaders and team members. Not all factors that affect us are controlled by any one person. This means sometimes limitations are inherited or imposed that are not necessarily just or deserved.

We will then focus on what is within our control, and not on those things beyond our ability to influence or change. We recognize that the most severe limitation is not a lack of labor, capital, or physical resources, but a lack of imagination and initiative. We will never be defeated as a team until we stop trying. All physical resources begin as intangible thoughts and beliefs. Therefore, by changing the ways we think, we can ultimately create new resources previously unavailable.

We acknowledge that sometimes what seems impossible really isn't and at other times the impossible is, indeed, impossible. We won't know the difference until we have attempted all challenges we encounter as achievable. Success is doing the best the team is capable of in any given circumstance. With that understanding, we have committed to succeed despite the difficulties, limitations, and setbacks we encounter.

BUCKING THE CONVENTIONAL WISDOM

Several years ago a Lockheed L1011 took off from the San Francisco airport. Shortly after takeoff, the pilots found themselves in an emergency situation: the nose of the airplane would not lower. Still flying at a low altitude and slow airspeed, the plane was certain to stall and crash unless something could be done. The crew played it by the book, trying everything they'd learned from years of instruction and experience. At one point the captain and co-pilot put their feet on the control yokes and pushed as hard as they could to muscle the nose down. The nose refused to lower.

In a last-ditch effort, the captain tried something that, according to the conventional wisdom, would prove disastrous: he reduced power. Normally, in this situation, reducing power causes the stall to occur more quickly. But mysteriously, the L1011 did not stall. Instead, the nose lowered and they landed the plane without injury. When the aircraft was examined, a mechanical deficiency inherent in all L1011s was discovered. The crew had helped avoid disaster for future flights as well.

Later the press challenged the captain on his decision to reduce power. They wanted to know why he had chosen a course of action known to be wrong. He replied, "When everything that's supposed to work doesn't work, the only thing left to do is what's not supposed to work."

Teambuilt organizations accept that there are times to buck the conventional wisdom. When you've done all the right things, and you're still not getting results, try breaking the rules. At that point, it's a risk worth taking. And sometimes, what appears to be foolishness is actually genius.

13

DEVELOPING THE TEAMBUILT DIFFERENCE

My first job right out of college was as an account executive at a publishing firm in a small community outside Milwaukee. In terms of salary and perks, it wasn't the best job I've ever held. But when it came to fun, pride, and camaraderie, I've never worked anywhere else, before or since, that came close to that job. I've often reflected on some of the differences that made Johnsonville Press such a great place to work.

Because the company was relatively small—about 100 people at the time—it was easy to get to know people and feel like part of the team. Even younger employees like myself had plenty of responsibility, more than they normally would have gotten at a larger corporation. People seemed turned on by the responsibility and fast-paced environment. We worked hard and often ate, drank, and played together after hours. I don't recall ever going through the formalities of teambuilding, and the team I'm referring to wasn't structured—it was simply made up of people who frequently worked together on projects. Given the nature of the work (target-marketed magazines used by corporate dealer networks and trade publications), the entire organization was so interdependent that teamwork was a necessity.

I recall a small incident that made a big difference to me. I was asked to join the company president and the director of marketing on a visit to a large Peterbilt truck dealer in Milwaukee that was using one of our targeted publications in a marketing program.

The president, at that time, was Larry Kem, a former McKinsey colleague and very successful businessman. I hadn't been an account executive with Johnsonville Press for very long, so I assumed my purpose on this trip was to watch quietly and learn.

That's why I still remember how the president introduced me. He could have introduced me any number of ways: account executive, new employee, or even assistant—all would have been accurate. Instead, what he said was, "Gentlemen, I'd like you to meet my *associate,* Mark Sanborn." I was impressed, because the term "associate" suggests respect and equality—although I was in no way the president's equal. With that introduction, he earned my complete loyalty and dedication.

But it took another, similar experience to make me fully appreciate the example Kem had set. Not long after our trip, I was giving a client a tour of Johnsonville Press. When it came time to introduce my secretary, who was a terrific person, I said, "This is Terri Brandt. She works for me."

I meant no disrespect. Still, it was a dumb introduction that Terri very diplomatically corrected. She said, "Mark, I work *with* you, not *for* you."

In retrospect, she summed up why there was such a strong spirit of partnership and teamwork at Johnsonville Press. We had clearly defined leadership that was providing direction. At the same time, we were thankfully free of an ego-driven hierarchy where people feuded over territorial issues. We knew what the company was trying to accomplish, and we worked with each other to get it done.

Johnsonville Press wasn't perfect. No company is. My recollection of working there isn't a romanticized version of what happened. I just remember knowing exactly what had to be done, being given a good deal of responsibility, being treated with respect, receiving support from management, and enjoying the people I worked with. I didn't know I would later devote several years to researching, developing, and presenting teamwork seminars, but I couldn't have asked for a better place to begin my education.

Since then I have studied and worked with literally hundreds of organizations as a professional speaker and consultant. Some were highly successful and recognized as industry leaders. Others were incredibly screwed up. Sometimes the differences in organizations were apparent. Other times, I had to search for them. But there are important differences between traditional and teambuilt organizations. I'd like to share some insights into six diverse organizations that have achieved *the teambuilt difference.*

The Professional Services Firm

BSW Group, Inc. is a professional services firm in Tulsa, Oklahoma, that helps clients develop building programs by providing land acquisition, architectural, civil engineering, and construction services. They specialize in serving clients with massive ongoing projects, such as Walmart, Hallmark, Marriott, and Tandy Corp. BSW completes more than 500 projects per year. That is akin to launching a space shuttle every business day—and two each on Saturdays and Sundays! *The Wall Street Journal,* in its 1989 Centennial Edition, picked BSW as one of the top 56 companies of the future. Certainly their way of doing business and the resulting successes are something most organizations would benefit from emulating. Productivity per employee is at least five times the industry average and BSW is able to provide high-quality services at competitive fees.

Their 160 employees, consisting of professionals and support staff, are organized into client-focused teams. There is one major team per client, but the total number of teams varies, depending on the number of programs a client has in progress. There are also internal support teams that include areas such as administration, accounting, risk management, and new business development.

Ask any of the three founding principals, David Broach, Bob Sober, and Bob Workman, the secret of their success and they are quick to credit each other and their employees. This is not false modesty, as demonstrated by their commitment to their employees. BSW's founders often refer to "the magnificence of our people." They continually examine working conditions, pay systems, individual education and training, and opportunities for growth, in an effort to create an environment that brings out that magnificence.

All employees, professional and support staff, share in the organization's success: 20 percent of corporate profits are returned to team members. BSW's training budget approaches $200,000 per year, or more than $1,000 per employee. Workman says, "You can get a lot of training for that kind of money." Employees attend Deming Quality seminars, participate in Tom Peters's *In Search of Excellence* program, and receive additional training depending upon interest and need.

Underlying all these efforts is a pervasive belief in the importance of employees and a perspective notably different from traditional management's. Workman explains, "One of the problems we've got in this country is the old black and white/right and wrong issue. The Japanese take a different approach. They search for 'the more desirable.' An action is not necessarily wrong, it's just less desirable than another action. The Japanese continue to look forward by focusing on continual, incremental improvement.

"It helps us at BSW not to focus on right or wrong so much. Because we focus on 'the more desirable' instead, our people are more willing to take risks.

"In any organization, including ours, there are relationships that are just starting and some that are ending. There are new projects with unknown potential, other projects that might typically be considered dogs, and some that are highly successful. *All of these things are necessary.* We don't focus just on the successful projects or worry about relationships that might be ending. Someday the new projects will replace the highly successful projects when they're no longer working. New relationships replace the ones that have ended. Even the dogs can become profitable if you have patience.

"At BSW it's OK if a team isn't performing to fiscal optimum. The operating principals ask themselves what's need to help the team improve. Have we given them sufficient support? Enough training and education? The technology they need? Effective marketing? Do we have the right people on the team? We take responsibility and say let's look at what *we* need to do."

To some, it may sound like anathema to say, "It's OK if a team isn't performing." But Workman's point isn't that teams aren't accountable for results. It's obvious that BSW's success has been driven by consistently high results. The point is that there is a shared responsibility between management and team members to get the team what it needs to win, the patience for it to happen, and the willingness to fail sometimes. Rather than placing blame, management shares responsibility. Rather than demanding instant pay-offs, they focus on long-term gains.

How can BSW's employee productivity be five times higher than their average competitor's? In part, it is because BSW designs quality into every step of their process. Teamwork, combined with highly sophisticated systems, create efficiencies that dramatically affect employee productivity and organizational profitability.

Their formula is both qualitative and quantitative—what they call a combination of high technology combined with the best people focused on quality. And they've found that none of those things are mutually exclusive of profit. "I never understood what my dad meant when he said 'you've got to spend money to make money' like I do now," says Workman, referring to BSW's ongoing investment in employees.

BSW Group, Inc. has captured the attention of their competitors and the business media with an unusual and successful way of doing business that's based on enlightened leadership and an unwavering commitment to their people. More important, these same things have captured the loyalty and dedication of the employees, who are the people who have made BSW teambuilt.

The Police Department

Team members are inspired by leaders who guide and direct rather than dictate. It is inspiring when a leader cares enough to ask and respects enough to listen.

One such leader is the police chief of La Habra, a town in Southern California. Isabel Mario, communications supervisor at the La Habra Police Department, shared this story of inspiring leadership. On November 19, 1990, a new police chief named Steven Staveley came on board. Employees were interested in how the new chief would assume control because enthusiasm in the department wasn't what it once had been. Could Chief Staveley rekindle that lost enthusiasm?

Everyone seemed impressed when the new chief made time to visit every employee personally. Visits were made during all different shifts. Staveley also sat in on briefings, toured the communications center, and listened to the dispatchers doing their jobs. Not only did he get the know team members, he took time to understand what they did.

Chief Staveley then sent out six cards, three blue and three white, to every full-time and part-time employee. On the blue cards he said, "I would like you to write down all the things you never want to see changed about this department." On the white cards: "Please write down the three things you'd like to see improved. Rank order them from most important to least important." When the cards were returned, and the responses tallied, 72 "needs improvement issues" had been suggested. A leadership team of captains, lieutenants, managers, sergeants, and supervisors refined them to a list of the five most pressing issues.

A department meeting was held and all the "needs improvement" and "never change this" issues were presented. The original raw data were shown so that everyone could see how much agreement there was on the "never change this" issues and how much diversity there was in the "needs improvement" areas. By March 1991, the department had begun to address the five major "needs improvement" issues as well as many of the smaller issues, while remaining mindful of the positive aspects that gave team members pride. A "we" rather then "me" approach is determining change and improvement in the department.

Employees have been inspired by this team approach to improvement, says Mario. Today she and many other employees feel empowered because they know there is someone in a high position who *knows them, understands them,* and *is willing to listen to them.* La Habra Police Department employees, under the leadership of Chief Staveley, have approached change as a teambuilt process.

The Glass Manufacturer

Donnelly Corp. is a manufacturer of quality auto mirrors, window systems, interior lights, and coated glass products worldwide. Founded in 1905 in Holland, Michigan, Donnelly employs 2,300 people and does $232 million in sales each year. The company has been profiled by the *Harvard Business Review* and included in the book *The 100 Best Companies to Work for in America.* They've received many awards and recognition from GM, Chrysler, Ford, Honda of America, Corning, and the governor of Michigan—just to name a few! One reason Donnelly earns praise is that the company started practicing participative management in 1951—fully 30 years before it was seriously considered by the rest of the business community.

Robert Levering, Milton Moskowitz, and Michael Katz, coauthors of *The 100 Best Companies to Work for in America,* said, "Donnelly operates on the notion that people can be responsible human beings, even in the workplace. They don't have to be *told* what to do; they can decide for themselves. The goal at this company is self-management."

An *Industry Week* profile of Donnelly in 1990 describes the importance of teamwork at this company. Donnelly uses a mix of self-directed and supervised work teams, and every employee is on a team. They try to keep team size at 20 to 25 people because larger groups hinder participation. Teams are involved in decision making, setting their own production goals (in conjunction with Donnelly's overall goals and objectives), electing their leader by team vote, and jointly determining pay scales with management to ensure compensation is competitive with that of nearby companies. A bonus plan shares profits with Donnelly employees, based on the company's total profitability.

Commitment to employees is further evidenced by a policy that no employee can be displaced by technology. Workers are given the opportunity to work in another area of the company if their jobs are eliminated because of process or technology improvements.

One of the ways Donnelly empowers employees is through a program called IDEAS, which stands for "Involved Donnelly Employees Achieve Success." The National Association of Suggestion Systems has recognized Donnelly for the financial success of this program two years in a row; 50 percent of all Donnelly employees participate. Lonnie Holmquist, who is in charge of the IDEAS program, says the key to identifying needs and filling them is asking employees these 10 questions:

1. What made you mad today?
2. What took too long?
3. What was the cause of any complaint?
4. What was misunderstood?
5. What cost too much?
6. What was wasted?
7. What was too complicated?
8. What was just plain silly?
9. What job took too many people?
10. What job involved too many actions?

Holmquist offers this warning about soliciting employee feedback: don't bother asking for suggestions unless you're prepared to do something about them. Participation in the IDEAS program is high because Donnelly doesn't just *ask;* they *respond* to employees' ideas and concerns.

The Ambulance Service

For seven of the past eight years, San Mateo County, California, located just south of San Francisco, was plagued with problems in their 911 emergency response service. The county was dealing with an ambulance service that had disgruntled employees, equipment that broke down, and relatively slow response times. So San Mateo County decided to seek bids for a new service—with a focus on quality rather than cost. The county awarded a contract to a company called BayStar, just 67 days prior to the implementation date. BayStar had to move fast.

The first thing BayStar management did was meet with the disgruntled, unionized paramedics. They discussed what was wrong and how to fix it. For the first time in their careers, these paramedics had managers who worked with them as a team. Together, they designed ambulances that are now the envy of the paramedic industry as well as a sophisticated computerized response system that changed their response times from some of the slowest to the fastest in the San Francisco Bay Area in less than one week. Compared with industry averages, BayStar's customers—victims of auto accidents, heart attacks, and other medical emergencies—are receiving some of the fastest treatment in the country.

There's a shortage of paramedics in the Bay Area, but teamwork and an upbeat, supportive corporate culture make staffing easy for BayStar. While other paramedic services in the area have full-time recruiters, BayStar's paramedics handle staffing themselves. When they needed to hire four new paramedics, BayStar was inundated with more than 70 applications. BayStar has the luxury of hiring only the best to work on their team.

Involving the paramedics in literally everything from ambulance design to new business ventures has helped develop their management and leadership skills. As a community project, two paramedics started an Explorer post to expose young people to emergency medicine. Within its first month, this project had built the largest Explorer post in the state of California.

As of this writing, BayStar has just celebrated its first anniversary. Their success has attracted international attention. EMS (Emergency Medical Service) leaders and managers from throughout the United States, England, and Australia have taken advantage of BayStar's open door and willingness to share what's worked for them. Greg

Gibson, publisher of an EMS magazine in Australia, says, "I've never seen anything like BayStar. They have paramedics in on everything and it works."

BayStar's eight corporate values, STAR CARE, are at the core of their teambuilt success. STAR CARE ensures that the care their customers receive will be:

> Safe
> Team-based
> Attentive to human needs
> Respectful
> Customer-accountable
> Appropriate
> Reasonable
> Ethical

Mike Taigman, who is in charge of quality improvement at BayStar, says he's amazed at what they were able to accomplish in such a short time by simply cooperating with employees, rather than competing against them to get the job done.

The BayStar story exemplifies many of the teambuilt principles in action: involving team members in decision making, which improves both quality and commitment to the decisions; accomplishing difficult assignments more quickly than thought possible; establishing a commitment to core values; and making the shift from competition to cooperation. In the process, they've found that success breeds success. BayStar has become the employer of choice for paramedics in an area suffering from paramedic shortages. Organizations that mistreat employees create a vicious circle: bad working conditions create bad morale, which makes working conditions even worse, eventually driving away good people. BayStar's use of teamwork has created a *victorious circle:* good working conditions attract good people, who create better working conditions, which attract better people.

The Software Company

Teamwork is a critical ingredient in the day-to-day operations at Software Publishing Corp. It is a part of their corporate culture. Their founder, Fred Gibbons, "grew up" at Hewlett Packard, where teamwork is "the HP way."

The Peer Achievement Award was introduced to provide recognition to individuals and teams whose performance goes measurably beyond standard expectations. Each quarter, nominations are solicited from throughout the company. Anyone who has demonstrated a passion for overachievement can be nominated by anyone else in the company, except his or her own manager. The nominations are reviewed by a committee that selects the three nominees who best exemplify overachievement. The three recipients each receive a $2,000 award at the quarterly company meeting, which is attended by the 500 employees at corporate headquarters. Sales Development Manager Bernie Borges says, "While the cash award is significant, it is not considered to be the primary motivation for the award. The prestige of the award is the fact that the recipient was nominated by their peers, just like the Pro Bowl in the NFL."

In the year that the Peer Achievement Award has been in place, SPC has learned some interesting things. The award is definitely not a popularity contest. The committee scrutinizes nominations carefully and does any research necessary to confirm that nominated employees are as outstanding as their nominators say they are. Many nominations are eliminated because they're merely examples of someone doing her or his job well. The objective is to recognize truly outstanding performance.

When the program was initiated, management anticipated that nominations would focus on individuals—but teams make up the vast majority of nominees and are most frequently selected as winners.

Borges says, "Even more interesting is that the teams nominated are not formal teams in the traditional sense. These teams are employees who are often in cross-functional groups, yet work closely together towards a common cause. In a recent example, a team won this award for banding together to create a market opportunity that was quite nontraditional for SPC. This team consisted of people from sales, marketing, finance, and operations. They met a challenge that appeared unattainable. In the end, they achieved their goal and created a profitable revenue opportunity for the company that would not have been achieved without the spirit of teamwork."

SPC is proof that, whether formal or informal, teamwork works.

The Utility Provider

The bulletin boards at Missouri Public Service display a steady stream of complimentary letters from customers. This is just one sign of recent improvements that have also resulted in a visible energy among the employees of this electric and natural gas utility, headquartered in Kansas City, Missouri. Company leadership credits a new work style that replaced rigid management with an open system that fosters teamwork and cooperation.

A continuous improvement process has been introduced to all of the utility's nearly 1,000 employees. Organized into a "Plan for Excellence," complete with objectives, strategies, and action plans, the crusade is lead by President Bob Green, whose vision is that the utility will become a recognized leader in the energy industry.

"Our industry is undergoing tremendous change," says Green. "Competition has never been a serious threat in this industry until the recent introduction of deregulation and open access. These two issues alone are causing us to rethink the way we do business."

The rethinking that went into the Plan for Excellence includes the introduction of new workplace philosophies such as teamwork, problem solving, benchmarking, and employee empowerment.

The power of employee teamwork and the creativity it inspires became evident in May 1991, when Missouri Public Service set a U.S. record of 177 days of continous operation at its Sibley electric generating station. Glenn Keefe, station superintendent at Sibley, says, "It's exciting to set a record, but more importantly, we're saving money for the company and our customers by operating this unit continuously.

"This plant couldn't operate without teamwork," says Keefe, who is convinced that every employee has good ideas and wants to contribute to the success of the organization. To that end, he actively solicits input from plant employees. "As station superintendent, I don't have all the answers. But as a team, we can tackle any challenge successfully."

Witness the team of maintenance welders at the Sibley plant who saved the company an estimated $100,000. It began when welder Larry Miller devised a shortcut for replacing a defective tube on a generating unit. Typically, this kind of tube replacement disables a unit for up to five days. During that time, power must be purchased from other utilities at an additional cost of $100,000 or more, depending on temperatures.

Miller suggested attaching a temporary replacement tube so the defective tube could be temporarily bypassed. Then when electricity demand dropped in the fall, the defective tube was replaced by Miller and his teammates. The generating unit was off-line for 37 hours of maintenance—rather than the usual 120 hours. "Even though the initial idea was one person's, it took everyone working together to complete the task," says Keefe.

At Missouri Public Service, a commitment to empowerment has translated pragmatically into problem solving and decision making. Tough issues once left to executives and upper management are now put before teams consisting of a variety of personnel throughout the company. President Green is adamant about their Plan for Excellence: "Today teamwork is part of our corporate culture. We're creating an environment that says to everyone, 'You're important to our success.' "

14

CONTINUING TO LEARN THE LESSON OF TEAMWORK

"There is nothing more difficult to plan,
more doubtful of success,
nor more dangerous to manage than the
creation of a new system."
Niccolò Machiavelli, The Prince

Machiavelli was a wet blanket. Sweeping social and organizational change is quite difficult, but becoming teambuilt is an undertaking with better odds. By reading this book, you've been exposed to many examples that prove the timeliness and benefits of teamwork. I've given you lots of ideas and practical techniques to try. Here comes the hard part:

So what are you going to do now?

IS IT POSSIBLE TO CHANGE?

Hegel, the German philosopher, said, "Man learns nothing from history." But the problem isn't our ability to *learn,* it's our ability to *remember.* We seem to learn a lesson only to promptly forget it. To change personally or organizationally, we must *keep learning*— when people are willing to do that, change is possible.

What drives organizational change? Probably the most common driver is crisis. We do what we have to do. Look at American automobile manufacturers. They built as fine an automobile as customers wanted—back when there was little foreign competition. One day Japan and Germany started gobbling up big chunks of marketshare, and guess what? American companies started building better cars. Why? Because they had to if they were to survive.

Isn't it amazing what organizations and industries can do when confronted with crisis? In the mid-'80s, when Ford decided to concentrate on building a world-class automobile, the company turned to teamwork. Ford's Taurus automobile was designed by a team that included designers, engineers, manufacturing employees, lawyers, marketers, dealers, suppliers, representatives of insurance companies, and customers. This cross-functional approach was a radical departure from the compartmentalized approach historically used in the design and manufacture of automobiles. And the resulting car was wildly successful: it sold like crazy, won accolades for design and quality, and came in under budget by almost one-half billion dollars.

Don't get sucked in by the doom-and-gloom crowd that says nothing ever changes. But avoid the complacent optimists as well. At a recent seminar, I was running through a list of challenges American business faces: declining productivity, poor standards of quality and service, and losing marketshare to foreign competitors. I used those problems to illustrate the need for change—not as fatalistic reasons to give up, as a doom-and-gloomer might.

At the end of the day, I got an evaluation from a complacent optimist who said: "Don't knock American business. After all, we're still No. 1!" (To that I would add, ". . . by a dramatically narrowing margin.")

Do we have to slip to No. 2 before we do anything differently? The biggest danger our country or your organization faces is terminal complacency, being content with past success. The optimistically complacent change only when faced with crisis. But they'll learn, just as the automobile industry did, that waiting until you *must* change in order to survive creates much wailing and gnashing of teeth. There is a rational alternative:

Change before crisis and pain necessitate it.

Somebody Has to Lead the Way

Don't wait for someone else to initiate teamwork. You don't have to be a manager to begin the teambuilt process. Regardless of your current position or influence, there is nothing to prevent you from creating a *teambuilt microcosm* within your group or organization.

Don't make any big announcements to anyone outside your group about what you're doing. Just implement the teambuilt concepts you've read about. When you have quantifiable results, that's the time to make your case for teamwork.

Don't be surprised if others ask you what you attribute your success to. When they notice a change in morale, improvement in productivity, or any number of teambuilt benefits, they'll get curious.

People are sold not so much by what they hear as by what they see.

Needed: Team Vigilantes, Evangelists and Positive Malcontents

If you're committed to making your organization teambuilt, you may need to be three things: a vigilante, an evangelist, and a positive malcontent.

A *vigilante* is "someone who keeps watch, especially to avoid danger." Vigilantes are usually self-appointed. As a team vigilante, you must keep watch for:

- opportunities to implement teambuilt concepts
- seeds of teamwork that need nurturing
- discouraged team members who need encouraging
- good news stories about how teamwork is working
- policies, procedures, and decisions that threaten the team concept
- influential team players in high places who can help advance the cause
- influential team slayers and skeptics who need to be sold

An *evangelist* has three jobs: proclaiming the gospel (in this case, the gospel of teamwork), converting nonbelievers, and equipping believers so they can share the news with others.

The unconverted need the influence of an evangelist. They need to spend time with someone who understands the practice of teamwork as well as its philosophy, and they need evidence to convert (that's why it's better to wait until you've gotten teambuilt results before telling others). Relationship building with others in your organization will be the foundation for future efforts to create teamwork.

Equipping believers is another important aspect of team evangelism. You can leverage your efforts by sharing your knowledge and findings with those who already believe—and will pass on the message. Believers need encouragement to stay sold.

A word of caution: It's harder to get better if you're already good. If your team or organization is mediocre, improvements and gains will be relatively easy to make. But if you're already excellent, improvements will come more slowly.

Likewise, if you've never attempted teamwork before, you should enjoy a few benefits immediately. But if you've been on the leading edge of implementing team concepts and are already enjoying results, future improvements will probably take longer and your gains will be incremental.

That's why you need a *positive malcontent*—a person who shakes the cage to keep others from becoming complacent. Being proud of what the team or organization has accomplished in the past is positive. Being content is negative. To keep growing, these two concepts must be fused: pride and discontent prevent complacency. That is the challenge of the positive malcontent, who raises such issues as:

- "Can we do it better?"
- "Why do it this way?"
- "What would happen if . . ."
- "What are we doing different this week?"
- "Good work—what have you planned for an encore?"
- "Let's try something different . . ."
- "We're not aiming high enough . . ."

START BY ASKING THE RIGHT QUESTION

Alert as a vigilante, skilled as an evangelist, and willing to play the positive malcontent, you're ready to lead the way to becoming teambuilt.

I'm afraid, however, that when you finish this book, in your well-intentioned enthusiasm for teamwork, you might be tempted to go back to your group and tell them what they're going to do to create teamwork. Don't forget:

Teamwork always begins with a question rather than a statement.

Chris Thomas is 32—younger than at least half the team he was asked to lead. Yet Thomas knew more about teamwork than any other leader in his organization by the time his management decided to implement self-managed teamwork. Thomas had attended the required team leader training sessions and had even gone on to study several books and videos on the topic. Certainly, he was well prepared to assume his position and make teamwork work.

Thomas could have set the agenda at the first team meeting by highlighting his plan for making his department teambuilt. But he knew that in doing so, he could easily arouse resentment and the contempt of experienced, valued employees who knew as much about the work to be done as he did.

The first team meeting was surprising to those in attendance. Thomas outlined the goals and objectives management had asked him to explain to the team. He talked about the benefits teamwork could produce for the group as well as individuals. Then he concluded the meeting with this request:

> "I cannot make teamwork work without your help. Together we know much more than any of us do individually. I would like you to fill in the blank in a statement I've had printed on the questionnaire each of you will receive. Please think carefully and return the questionnaire within the next two days. Together, we will address what you suggest."

The questionnaire contained a single statement:

> *"If I were the leader of this team, I would* _____."

Thomas had demonstrated his understanding of teamwork and the importance of involvement. He spent the next several months following up on his team members' suggestions and helping them achieve their shared agenda.

JUST DO IT

Former president Calvin Coolidge once said, "We cannot do everything at once, but we must do something at once." Once you get your group to come up with an agenda, the next challenge you face is trying to do everything at once. Attempt too much and you'll be overwhelmed. Attempt nothing and you'll lose credibility.

The "rule of three" will help you prioritize your team agenda. The rule asks this question:

What three things, if we accomplished them, would produce the biggest payback on our team's investment of time and energy?

Three is a manageable number that allows the team to focus its attention and energies. Now it's time for action planning.

Achieving significant long-term goals requires immediate and consistent short-term wins. Once you've identified your three accomplishments, break them down into small and immediately executable action steps. These steps become your QTWs (Quick Team Wins). Remember, QTWs create a momentum toward success by giving team members specific things they can do immediately that will provide positive reinforcement.

You've focused the team's attention, strategized a plan, and identified QTWs. The only thing left: *just do it.*

If you lead the way to becoming teambuilt, don't be discouraged by your inability to create immediate change. Change is possible, but I never claimed it was easy or quick. Don't get caught up in trying to help everyone and change everything—because you can't. What is exciting is that *you can help someone* and *you can change some-*

thing. All it takes is getting started. Once you've done that, it's a matter of continuing to learn the teamwork lesson.

THE LESSON OF TEAMWORK

The lesson of teamwork became very clear to me in 1986 on a raft trip down the Colorado River. I went with a group of more than 30 people: speakers and their families and friends. We started in Page, Arizona, in three rafts and spent the next eight days covering 220 miles of the most spectacular river and scenery anywhere.

I think it is safe to generalize that speakers are a rather assertive and competitive bunch by nature. At least our group was, and we soon developed an informal competition on the river.

Every few days, we would come to a waterfall either on the river or in a side canyon. If you've ever explored a waterfall, you know that behind most falls is a cave-like area hollowed out by the turbulent water. The size of these little caves varies, but usually they are big enough for one or two people to stand inside. But you've got to get through the rushing water to enjoy this unique insider's view. So we began to compete to see who could be the first to penetrate the falls.

It was near the end of the trip when we came to the biggest fall of all. Water was cascading down, hitting a pool below with incredible velocity. The waterfall was loud, windy, and very powerful.

Several of us tried unsuccessfully to penetrate the fall. The water was ice cold and so turbulent that anyone who got close was thrown back. Still, some of us knocked ourselves silly trying.

Our trip leader was a professional guide who had been down the Colorado many times. He finally spoke up and told us that in all his years of running the river, nobody had ever penetrated this particular waterfall. In fact, on his last trip, a group of big guys had joined hands and tried to do it as a team. They, too, had failed. But we had some creative people in our group. Someone suggested that we lock elbows and form a circle because the structural rigidity of an unbroken circle might allow us to penetrate the fall.

I remember this vividly because I was part of that crazy team. I'm not a little guy by most standards, but there were people in this group who were much taller and stockier than I. On my right, I locked elbows with Al Walker, a speaker from South Carolina, who is a big man. On my left, I locked elbows with Ed Grief, a speaker from Kansas City, who is very tall. I learned an interesting lesson that day about commitment: *when you lock elbows with people who are bigger than you, you are committed.*

All facing inward, this tight little group started moving toward the fall. It was wild. The water was getting deeper and more violent the closer we got. It even seemed to be getting colder.

When we reached the point where we could move no farther, we were directly under the waterfall, not inside it. Water was coming down on my head like a jackhammer and bubbling back up my nose. Suddenly philosophical, I began to consider the question, "How long can the human body go without oxygen?"

I was ready to leave but Ed and Al each had a death grip on my elbows, and they were holding their ground. It was getting intense when suddenly I felt the circle start to weaken, and next thing I knew, we were thrown back.

A quick head count showed that one of our team was missing. It was a little scary. Being a world-class worrier, I began to think we'd drowned a member of our group in our attempt to penetrate the waterfall. We were searching the water frantically when suddenly the missing person came bursting through the fall, hands over his head in triumph, yelling, "I did it! I was in! I was in!"

The victorious rafter was a teenager named John. When he calmed down, he explained how he had done it. When the circle had stopped, unable to go any farther, John was in front. He was close

216

enough to see that there was a space behind the waterfall just big enough for one person. So he released, pushed off the circle, and was able to make it all the way into the cave. As far as we know, John was the first person to ever penetrate that waterfall.

It would be fun if I could relate that story with a different ending, and tell you *I* was the one who penetrated the waterfall—but I didn't. Still, I got just as big a thrill being part of the team that helped John succeed as if I had done it myself. That day, on the Colorado River, the lesson of teamwork became very real to me. It is a lesson we need to continue learning in our organizations and communities, and as cohabitants of this planet:

> *You always accomplish more cooperating with people*
> *than you do competing against them.*

That is the lesson of teamwork.

ABOUT THE AUTHOR

Mark Sanborn has built an international reputation among businesses and organizations as "the high-content speaker who motivates." An authority on teambuilding, leadership and service, he presents more than 100 speeches and seminars annually. His clients include such leading corporations and organizations as AT&T, Merck, Pepsi, United Artists, Hallmark, The Coast Guard, United Way and the American Hospital Association.

Author of numerous audio and video training programs, including *High-Impact Leadership: How to Be More than a Manager* and *Team Building: How to Motivate and Manage People,* Sanborn has also been featured on *Manager's Edge,* an audio cassette program heard monthly by more than 14,000 managers.

Mark Sanborn lives in Denver.

Additional copies of *Teambuilt: Making Teamwork Work* may be ordered by sending a check for $19.95 (please add the following for postage and handling: $2.00 for the first copy, $1.00 for each added copy) to:

MasterMedia Limited
17 East 89th Street
New York, NY 10128
(212) 260-5600
(800) 334-8232
fax: (212) 348-2020

Mark Sanborn is available for speeches and seminars. Please contact MasterMedia's Speakers' Bureau for availability and fee arrangements. Call Tony Colao at (800) 4-LECTUR, or fax: (908) 359-1647.

OTHER MASTERMEDIA BOOKS

THE PREGNANCY AND MOTHERHOOD DIARY: Planning the First Year of Your Second Career, by Susan Schiffer Stautberg, is the first and only undated appointment diary that shows how to manage pregnancy and career. ($12.95 spiralbound)

CITIES OF OPPORTUNITY: Finding the Best Place to Work, Live and Prosper in the 1990's and Beyond, by Dr. John Tepper Marlin, explores the job and living options for the next decade and into the next century. This consumer guide and handbook, written by one of the world's experts on cities, selects and features forty-six American cities and metropolitan areas. ($13.95 paper, $24.95 cloth)

THE DOLLARS AND SENSE OF DIVORCE, by Dr. Judith Briles, is the first book to combine practical tips on overcoming the legal hurdles with planning finances before, during, and after divorce. ($10.95 paper)

OUT THE ORGANIZATION: New Career Opportunities for the 1990s, by Robert and Madeleine Swain, is written for the millions of Americans whose jobs are no longer safe, whose companies are not loyal, and who face futures of uncertainty. It gives advice on finding a new job or starting your own business. ($12.95 paper)

AGING PARENTS AND YOU: A Complete Handbook to Help You Help Your Elders Maintain a Healthy, Productive and Independent Life, by Eugenia Anderson-Ellis, is a complete guide to providing care to aging relatives. It gives practical advice and resources to the adults who are helping their elders lead productive and independent lives. ($9.95 paper)

CRITICISM IN YOUR LIFE: How to Give It, How to Take It, How to Make It Work for You, by Dr. Deborah Bright, offers practical advice, in an upbeat, readable, and realistic fashion, for turning criticism into control. Charts and diagrams guide the reader into managing criticism from bosses, spouses, relationships, children, friends, neighbors, and in-laws. ($17.95 cloth)

BEYOND SUCCESS: How Volunteer Service Can Help You Begin Making a Life Instead of Just a Living, by John F. Raynolds III and Eleanor Raynolds, C.B.E., is a unique how-to book targeted to business and professional people considering volunteer work, senior citizens who wish to fill leisure time meaningfully, and students trying out various career options. The book is filled with interviews with celebrities, CEOs, and average citizens who talk about the benefits of service work. ($19.95 cloth)

MANAGING IT ALL: Time-Saving Ideas for Career, Family, Relationships, and Self, by Beverly Benz Treuille and Susan Schiffer Stautberg, is written for women who are juggling careers and families. Over two hundred career women (ranging from a TV anchorwoman to an investment banker) were interviewed. The book contains many humorous anecdotes on saving time and improving the quality of life for self and family. ($9.95 paper)

YOUR HEALTHY BODY, YOUR HEALTHY LIFE: How to Take Control of Your Medical Destiny, by Donald B. Louria, M.D., provides precise advice and strategies that will help you to live a long and healthy life. Learn also about nutrition, exercise, vitamins and medication, as well as how to control risk factors for major diseases. ($12.95 paper)

THE CONFIDENCE FACTOR: How Self-Esteem Can Change Your Life, by Judith Briles, is based on a nationwide survey of six thousand men and women. Briles explores why women so often feel a lack of self-confidence and have a poor opinion of themselves. She offers step-by-step advice on becoming the person you want to be. ($9.95 paper, $18.95 cloth)

THE SOLUTION TO POLLUTION: 101 Things You Can Do to Clean Up Your Environment, by Laurence Sombke, offers step-by-step techniques on how to conserve more energy, start a recycling center, choose biodegradable products and proceed with individual environmental cleanup projects. ($7.95 paper)

TAKING CONTROL OF YOUR LIFE: The Secrets of Successful Enterprising Women, by Gail Blanke and Kathleen Walas, is based on the authors' professional experience with Avon Products' Women of Enterprise Awards, given each year to outstanding women entrepreneurs. The authors offer a specific plan to help you gain control over your life and include business tips and quizzes as well as beauty and lifestyle information. ($17.95 cloth)

SIDE-BY-SIDE STRATEGIES: How Two-Career Couples Can Thrive in the Nineties, by Jane Hershey Cuozzo and S. Diane Graham, describes how two-career couples can learn the difference between competing with a spouse and becoming a supportive power partner. Published in hardcover as *Power Partners.* ($10.95 paper, $19.95 cloth)

DARE TO CONFRONT! How to Intervene When Someone You Care About Has an Alcohol or Drug Problem, by Bob Wright and Deborah George Wright, shows the reader how to use the step-by-step methods of professional interventionists to motivate drug-dependent people to accept the help they need. ($17.95 cloth)

WORK WITH ME! How to Make the Most of Office Support Staff, by Betsy Lazary, shows how to find, train, and nurture the "perfect" assistant and how best to utilize your support staff professionals. ($9.95 paper)

MANN FOR ALL SEASONS: Wit and Wisdom from The Washington Post*'s Judy Mann,* by Judy Mann, shows the columnist at her best as she writes about women, families and the politics of the women's revolution. ($9.95 paper, $19.95 cloth)

THE SOLUTION TO POLLUTION IN THE WORKPLACE, by Laurence Sombke, Terry M. Robertson and Elliot M. Kaplan, supplies employees with everything they need to know about cleaning up their workspace, including recycling, using energy efficiently, conserving water and buying recycled products and nontoxic supplies. ($9.95 paper)

THE ENVIRONMENTAL GARDENER: The Solution to Pollution for Lawns and Gardens, by Laurence Sombke, focuses on what each of us can do to protect our endangered plant life. A practical sourcebook and shopping guide. ($8.95 paper)

THE LOYALTY FACTOR: Building Trust in Today's Workplace, by Carol Kinsey Goman, Ph.D., offers techniques for restoring commitment and loyalty in the workplace. ($9.95 paper)

DARE TO CHANGE YOUR JOB—AND YOUR LIFE, by Carole Kanchier, Ph.D., provides a look at career growth and development throughout the life cycle. ($10.95 paper)

MISS AMERICA: In Pursuit of the Crown, by Ann-Marie Bivans, is an authorized guidebook to the Pageant, containing eyewitness accounts, complete historical data, and a realistic look at the trials and triumphs of potential Miss Americas. ($27.50 cloth)

POSITIVELY OUTRAGEOUS SERVICE: New and Easy Ways to Win Customers for Life, by T. Scott Gross, identifies what the consumers of the nineties really want and how businesses can develop effective marketing strategies to answer those needs. ($14.95 paper)

BREATHING SPACE: Living and Working at a Comfortable Pace in a Sped-Up Society, by Jeff Davidson, helps readers to handle information and activity overload and gain greater control over their lives. ($10.95 paper)

TWENTYSOMETHING: Managing and Motivating Today's New Work Force, by Lawrence J. Bradford, Ph.D., and Claire Raines, M.A., examines the work orientation of the younger generation, offering managers in businesses of all kinds a practical guide to better understand and supervise their young employees. ($22.95 cloth)

BALANCING ACTS! Juggling Love, Work, Family and Recreation, by Susan Schiffer Stautberg and Marcia L. Worthing, provides strategies to achieve a balanced life by reordering priorities and setting realistic goals. ($12.95 paper)

THE LIVING HEART BRAND NAME SHOPPER'S GUIDE, by Michael E. DeBakey, M.D., Antonio M. Gotto, Jr., M.D., D.Phil., Lynne W. Scott, M.A., R.D./L.D., and John P. Foreyt, Ph.D., lists brand-name supermarket products that are low in fat, saturated fatty acids, and cholesterol. ($12.95 paper)

STEP FORWARD: Sexual Harassment in the Workplace, What You Need to Know, by Susan L. Webb, teaches the reader the facts about sexual harassment and furnishes procedures to help stop it. ($9.95 paper)

REAL LIFE 101: The Graduate's Guide to Survival, by Susan Kleinman, supplies welcome advice to those facing "real life" for the first time, focusing on work, money, health, and how to deal with freedom and responsibility. ($9.95 paper)

A TEEN'S GUIDE TO BUSINESS: The Secrets to a Successful Enterprise, by Linda Menzies, Oren S. Jenkins, and Rickell R. Fisher, provides solid information about starting your own business or working for one. ($7.95 paper)

THE OUTDOOR WOMAN: A Handbook to Adventure, by Patricia Hubbard and Stan Wass, details the lives of adventurous outdoor women and offers their ideas on how you can incorporate exciting outdoor experiences into your life. ($14.95 paper)

REAL BEAUTY . . . REAL WOMEN: A Workbook for Making the Best of Your Own Good Looks, by Kathleen Walas, International Beauty and Fashion Director of Avon Products, offers expert advice on beauty and fashion to women of all ages and ethnic backgrounds. ($19.50 paper)

MANAGING YOUR CHILD'S DIABETES, by Robert Wood Johnson IV, Sale Johnson, Casey Johnson, and Susan Kleinman, brings help to families trying to understand diabetes and control its effects. ($10.95 paper)

GLORIOUS ROOTS: Recipes for Healthy, Tasty Vegetables, by Laurence Sombke, celebrates the taste, texture, and versatility of root vegetables. Contains recipes for appetizers, soups, stews, baked, boiled, and stir-fried dishes— even desserts. ($14.95 paper)

DATE DUE

DEC 1 1 2000		
5/16/07		
29694648		

Demco, Inc. 38-293